Praise for
The Jewish Wedding Now

"I know you. You wish you already knew someone who would explain what's what in Jewish wedding land. Someone who loves the gorgeous Jewish tradition and all that it offers. Someone who also gets that the modern world is actually a tremendous asset. Someone who has good taste and isn't afraid to say it like it is. Well, your wish came true. Anita Diamant is that person, and *The Jewish Wedding Now* is all you need. I pray all your wedding dramas get resolved so easily."

—Rabbi Noa Kushner, founding rabbi of
The Kitchen, a religious start-up in San Francisco,
www.thekitchensf.org.

"No two weddings are alike, and in *The Jewish Wedding Now* Anita Diamant has spot-on advice for every couple—from the most traditional to the most cutting edge. Whether your wedding is interfaith, LGBTQ, very observant or just Jewish, she will walk you through every step of this emotionally fraught, ritually complex and spiritually fertile life-cycle moment. Without judging what couples should choose or avoid, Diamant explains, teaches, describes, and inspires."

—Rabbi Rick Jacobs,
president,
Union for Reform Judaism

"I have recommended Anita Diamant's earlier editions of *The Jewish Wedding Now* to countless couples I've married for twenty-five years. This newest edition is in many ways more a new book than just an update. Diamant takes on the realities of Jewish life as it really is—with depth and sensitivity. LGBTQ, multifaith, Jews-of-color are present in the fullness of who we are—not only as apologetic add-ons. Issues of complicated family structures at weddings are confronted directly. Divorce is an acknowledged reality in our communities and families. Kudos to Anita Diamant! This book will serve the Jewish community—as we truly are—well!"

—Rabbi Sharon Kleinbaum,
DD, senior rabbi,
Congregation Beit Simchat Torah, New York

"Anita Diamant has given us a gift with *The Jewish Wedding Now*, which refreshingly offers us depth, inclusivity, and accessibility. This is a must-read for Jewish couples planning their special day to be cherished forever!"

—Rabbi Dr. Shmuly Yanklowitz,
founder and president,
Uri L'Tzedek: Orthodox Social Justice

"This revised version of a beloved classic offers an accessible, diverse, and sensitive guide for Jews who love and those who love them to create meaningful weddings and marriages. It's not just a book about love, it's a book about making love and life matter more in a fast-changing world."

—Rabbi Amichai Lau-Lavie,
founder of Lab/Shul, New York,
www.labshul.org

"*The Jewish Wedding Now* is a precious resource, revealing the spiritual gifts of Jewish wedding traditions to a wider community of loving partners and ritual practitioners. LGBTQ families and interfaith families should be embraced by Jewish tradition, and Anita Diamant's words (and heart) open the door to Jewish wisdom as wide as it was always meant to be. With this new gift from one of the world's most eloquent, sensitive teachers, a couple's celebration might end up transforming the entire world. To couples hoping to create a meaningful wedding, individual spiritual seekers, and ritual facilitators of every variety, I cannot recommend *The Jewish Wedding Now* highly enough!"

—Rabbi Menachem Creditor,
Congregation Netivot Shalom,
Berkeley, California

ALSO BY ANITA DIAMANT

FICTION
The Boston Girl
Day After Night
The Last Days of Dogtown
Good Harbor
The Red Tent

NONFICTION
How to Raise a Jewish Child
Living a Jewish Life
The New Jewish Baby Book
Pitching My Tent (Essays)
Saying Kaddish: How to Mourn as a Jew
Choosing a Jewish Life:
A Handbook for People Converting to Judaism
and for Their Family and Friends

The
JEWISH
WEDDING
Now

Anita Diamant

SCRIBNER

NEW YORK   LONDON   TORONTO   SYDNEY   NEW DELHI

Scribner
An Imprint of Simon and Schuster
1230 Avenue of the Americas
New York, NY 10020

Copyright © 1985, 2001, 2017 by Anita Diamant

Third edition. First Scribner edition June 2017

Scribner and design are registered trademarks of The Gale Group, Inc., used under license by Simon & Schuster, Inc., the publisher of this work.

For information about special discounts for bulk purchases, please contact Simon & Schuster Special Sales at 1-866-506-1949 or business@simonandschuster.com.

The Simon & Schuster Speakers Bureau can bring authors to your live event. For more information or to book an event, contact the Simon & Schuster Speakers Bureau at 1-866-248-3049 or visit our website at www.simonspeakers.com.

Designed by Maura Fadden Rosenthal/Mspace

Manufactured in the United States of America

10 9 8 7 6

Library of Congress Control Number: 00-049502

ISBN 978-1-5011-5394-5 (pbk)

Permissions for this book appear on page 211.

For Jim
my beloved, my friend

בס״ד

בשנת חמשת אלפים ושבע מאות שישים ושמונה לבריאת העולם

ה שבט כ״ח

On the second day of the week, the twenty-eighth day of the month of Shevat in the year 5768, corresponding to the fourth day of February in the year 2008 here in Upper Nyack, New York, USA, in the presence of family and friends, the beloveds Abe Franklin, son of Sylvia and Frank Franklin, and Sarah Freedman, daughter of Norman and Leah Freedman, entered into the covenant of marriage.

As we embark on life's journey, we promise to love, cherish, encourage and inspire one another. Our hearts fuse together, creating a unique bond with friendship and compassion at its core. Through this union, we vow to value and support each other, always striving to show sensitivity to each other's needs. We shall nurture one another emotionally, spiritually and intellectually, always mindful of our respective qualities and strengths. May we continue to grow together, maintaining the courage and determination to pursue our desired paths. We promise to celebrate life's joys with grace and overcome life's adversities with tenacity. May we maintain the intimacy that fosters trust, honesty and communication. As life partners, we shall strive to build a home emanating love, peace, tolerance and charity. Through each other's eyes, we see the world anew: may we be better together. All this is valid and binding.

Witness _____ עד
Witness _____ עד
Rabbi _____ חייב
Bride _____ כמלה
Groom _____ התווק

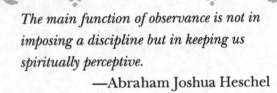

The main function of observance is not in imposing a discipline but in keeping us spiritually perceptive.

—Abraham Joshua Heschel

CONTENTS

AFTERWARD

APPENDICES

PREFACE
TO THE THIRD EDITION

When *The New Jewish Wedding* was first published in 1985, most American Jews knew little about the traditions and customs that have distinguished Jewish weddings for centuries: the *ketubah*—the Jewish marriage certificate—was a rabbinic formality at best; klezmer music was a corny exercise in nostalgia; just the words *Jewish wedding* summoned the vanished world of *Fiddler on the Roof* or the extravagant excess of *Goodbye, Columbus*.

The second edition of *The New Jewish Wedding* came out in 2001, when klezmer had achieved the status of funky/cool roots music and Jewish calligraphers and graphic designers had reclaimed the *ketubah* for a new generation and made it universally available on the Internet. The second edition also reflected the full inclusion of women in all aspects of Jewish life and the community's emerging embrace of its own diversity.

As in past editions, this one features contemporary art, liturgy, translations, and resources to inform and inspire meaningful Jewish choices. But it also reflects profound changes in American Jewry. While Ashkenazi culture is still dominant, there is new appreciation for the rituals, cuisines, music, and customs of other Jewish communities around the world. Jews of color, LGBTQ Jews, and those with roots in other countries and cultures enlarge and enrich the range of Jewish experiences and choices for everyone.

There is also a shift away from the hyphenated Judaism of past generations; boundaries between denominations are less distinct and affiliation rates are lower. The advent of an "open Orthodoxy" has started a new conversation about the differences between liberal and orthodox Judaism. Many prefer not to apply labels and describe themselves as post-denominational or "just Jewish."

The world has become a smaller place, but the huppah, the wedding canopy, has become a very large tent, open to Jews of all descriptions and denominations, and to people unconnected to any religion ("nones"),* "Jews by affiliation" (those who are in effect marrying in),† and people from different faith traditions. The status and validity of some of these weddings is the subject of intense debate—par for the course in all things Jewish—but this edition reflects the facts on the ground.

I hope that readers of all descriptions will find ideas, information, and a warm welcome in its pages; to that end, the language in this edition reflects a more expansive notion of gender, both in its use of pronouns (*they* rather than *he/she*), and in most cases *couples* and *beloveds* rather than *brides and grooms*, although even those words may now be understood as inclusive of "brides and brides"

---

* *Nones* is a term from surveys of religious affiliation where "none" or "none of the above" is one of the choices.
† See page 14 for more about "Jews by affiliation."

and "grooms and grooms." There is no chapter devoted to LGBTQ couples nor is there one for intermarrying couples because *The Jewish Wedding Now* is a menu for all who wish to include meaningful Jewish choices as they plan their ceremony and celebration: choices that are the same for everyone. As in past editions, it assumes the reader's interest and intelligence, but no experience or knowledge of vocabulary, customs, and laws. And while its purpose remains the same, I wondered whether it was time to reconsider the title. Thirty years on, has change outstripped continuity? Can *The New Jewish Wedding* still be *new*?

After much thought I decided to call this edition *The Jewish Wedding Now*. Under the *huppah*, time dissolves. All the lists and decisions about where, when, what to wear, whom to invite: it all recedes into a radical *now*. Your wedding takes place in the same time zone as the first wedding, when God braided Eve's hair and stood with Adam as a witness. Your wedding is the first wedding in the world and it is also the ultimate wedding—the latest chapter in a story that extends back four thousand years and will continue into the unknowable future.

I hope this book will help you create that crazy-sacred *now* at the heart of every wedding when two people under the *huppah* publicly declare that what they want for their "only wild and precious"* lives is to share it with each other.

Wishing you a joyful wedding and a long and happy marriage.

Mazel tov.

---

* Mary Oliver.

Shin Washi Paper Ketubah
© Temma Gentles
Image courtesy of www.ketubah.com

Introduction

According to Jewish law, the *requirements* for a kosher* wedding can be summed up in a few words: a bride accepts an object worth more than a dime from a groom; the groom recites a ritual formula to consecrate the transaction; these actions must be witnessed by two people who are not related to either bride or groom. That's it.

The *traditions* associated with Jewish weddings—the canopy, the breaking of a glass, the presence of a rabbi, even the seven wedding blessings—are customs. Custom—in Hebrew, *minhag*—changes over time and differs among cultures, nations, and generations; customs can vary wildly from one synagogue or neighborhood to the next.

Customs are not trivial; they are the heart and soul of rituals, and while some *minhagim* have been discarded and forgotten, others persist and carry even more symbolic and emotional weight than some religious requirements. Customs are not set in stone. Over the centuries Jewish weddings have been celebrated with variations in ritual and *minhag* that reflected the needs and values of different times and places.

---

* "Proper/legitimate." All Hebrew and Yiddish words are translated and defined at least once in the text and also appear in the glossary.

The nostalgic fallacy that there was once a standard, universal, and correct way to do a Jewish wedding ignores differences in everything from clothes to the fact that for centuries some Jews practiced polygamy.

Throughout history, Judaism has been a living tradition, examined, debated, and reinvented, generation after generation. Jewish weddings are grounded in the past, but they have always been the stuff of the irrepressible present.

This history of dynamic change is just as Jewish as the *huppah* and the seven wedding blessings. Yet, this kind of book would have been unthinkable before the twentieth century. Until then, most Jews lived in close-knit, homogenous communities. Families were as generous and hospitable as their means allowed, but ceremonies and celebrations—from the words spoken under the wedding canopy to the menu—were familiar to everyone.

Today, communities are scattered, culturally diverse, and even virtual. We don't share a common ritual language, and many of us have never been to a Jewish wedding. Our celebrations are mounted by professionals, whose main focus is on the reception, not what goes on under the *huppah*. There is a lot of hand-wringing and breast-beating about how this represents a terrible loss. But the truth is, Jews of the twenty-first century cannot marry the same way their parents did, much less their great-grandparents. The world has changed too much; our expectations of marriage are not the same. To be emotionally and spiritually authentic, our weddings need to synthesize the sum total of our experience, which includes the reality of our daily lives.

To make a wedding that is both authentically Jewish

and personally meaningful requires a level of conscious decision making that would have mystified previous generations: Should we use Hebrew words in the wedding invitation? How do we arrange the processional with two sets of divorced parents in the mix? What do we want our *ketubah* to say?

How are we going to make our wedding Jewish? How Jewish are we going to make our wedding?

The more numerous the choices, the greater the likelihood of disagreements. The Yiddish proverb "No *ketubah* was ever signed without an argument" was addressed to family squabbles (still a reality), but it also applies to the friction between tradition and personal style, between a four-thousand-year-old system of laws and contemporary values about, among other things, women's roles. Transforming that heat into light is the challenge of making Jewish tradition your own, and the purpose of *The Jewish Wedding Now*.

The Jewish Wedding Now includes ancient stories and texts from the Bible, the Talmud, Midrash, and mystical sources; examples of traditional liturgy and documents; contemporary prayers, translations, reimagined rituals, and documents; examples from Judaism's historic, religious, gastronomic, musical, and literary traditions.

The result of all this learning, choosing, and even arguing is more than a glorious party. As rites of passage, weddings clarify and express a lot about the people under the *huppah*. A wedding is a public announcement and demonstration of who you are as a couple. When you draw on Jewish tradition—borrowing, revising, even rejecting— the tradition becomes yours. And it lives.

The
JEWISH
WEDDING
Now

Mexican Plate Ketubah
© Ginny Reel
Image courtesy of www.ketubah-arts.com

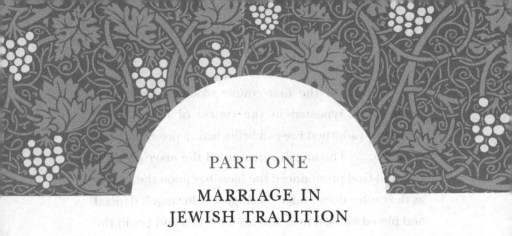

PART ONE
MARRIAGE IN
JEWISH TRADITION

Judaism sanctifies every dimension and chapter of human life with rituals, laws, and blessings. The very first of the 613 *mitzvot* (commandments) in the Torah is "Be fruitful and multiply," which was understood as a mandate to marry and help create the next generation.

Marriage is seen as the prototypical act of creation. The Zohar, the great book of Jewish mysticism, states, "God creates new worlds constantly. In what way? By causing marriages to take place."[1] The Talmud records that "one who does not participate in 'be fruitful and multiply' causes God's presence to vanish."[2] The wedding is equated with the two peak moments in the sacred experience of the Jewish people; both the covenant at Sinai and the joy of Shabbat are described in terms of the union of bride and groom. Heaven itself was preoccupied with marriage. According to the Talmud, "Forty days before the formation of a child, a voice proclaims in heaven, 'So-and-so's daughter is to marry so-and-so's son.'"[3]

The imaginative rabbinic commentary known as Midrash places God at the first wedding:

The wedding of the first couple was celebrated with pomp never repeated in the course of history. God attired and adorned Eve as a bride before presenting her to Adam. . . . The angels surrounded the marriage canopy, and God pronounced the blessings upon the couple as the cantor does under the *huppah*. The angels danced and played musical instruments for Adam and Eve in the ten bridal chambers of gold, pearls, and precious stones that God had prepared for them.[4]

The Midrash also portrays God as a universal matchmaker:

A wealthy Roman matron asked Rabbi Jose bar Halafta, "How long did it take the Holy One, blessed be He, to create the world?"

He said to her, "Six days."

"From then until now what has He been doing?"

"The Holy One, blessed be He, is occupied in making marriages."

The matron was unimpressed. "Even I can do that," she said, and set out to prove her point.

She placed a thousand male slaves and a thousand female slaves in rows and paired them off. The next day they came before her bruised and furious, saying, "I do not want the one you gave me."

The woman sent for Rabbi Jose bar Halafta and said, "Rabbi, your Torah is true, beautiful, and praiseworthy."

Rabbi Jose bar Halafta was not surprised. "A suitable match may seem easy to make, but God considers it as difficult a task as dividing the Sea of Reeds."[5]

Nor does God disappear from a marriage after a match is made:

> Adam's original name was esh—fire; Eve was also called esh. But when they married, two of the letters of God's name (Yud-Hay-Vav-Hay) were added to each of theirs. Adam's name became aleph-Yud-shin, ish—man, and Eve's name became aleph-shin-Hay, ishah—woman. Thus when God's presence is absent from a marriage, there is only esh and esh, "fire consuming fire."[6]

Although the rabbis considered marriage divine in origin and a holy obligation, they understood it was a human enterprise, subject to difficulties and even failure. Much of the Talmudic tractate *Nashim* (women) is devoted to laws concerning marriage, including dowries, the responsibilities of wives and husbands, sexual conduct, and divorce—laws that are complex, sometimes contradictory, and undeniably patriarchal.

The commandment to marry is directed toward men. According to the Talmud, a wife can save a young man from "sinful thoughts,"[7] and "any man who has no wife is not a man."[8] Marriage to a good woman is described as the source of happiness and blessing for a man.

Halachah does not accord women and men the same legal standing. As a legal agreement, a wedding must include an act of transaction: *kinyan*, a word that means "acquire." The groom acquires the bride by presenting her with a ring and saying the *haray aht*: "With this ring I consecrate myself to you according to the laws of Moses and

Israel." The bride must freely accept the ring, but she need not say or do anything else.

Although the Talmud reflects a patriarchal view of women as property, it did assign them some rights that were, for its time, progressive: minor girls could not be betrothed, and women had the legal right to refuse any suitor regardless of her family's wishes. Conjugal rape was prohibited, and although only men could grant divorces, women were entitled to sue for divorce on certain grounds, including sexual incompatibility. Men are also repeatedly instructed to treat women with respect and tenderness or risk divine wrath.

Judaism's insistence on marriage for everyone was, in its way, democratic. The community was obliged to help find mates for all of its members, regardless of status, class, physical appearance, or able-bodied-ness. Judaism affirmed sexuality as a human need and rejected celibacy as a form of religious commitment. It also viewed marriage as an essential source of human happiness, which tended to elevate the status of women within the home. In many homes, it was customary for husbands to recite or sing *"Eshet Chayil"*—"A Woman of Valor"—to their wives (See page 187). This poem, based on verses from Proverbs, is a list of virtues that includes intelligence and skill as well as kindness and generosity.

Although having children was considered the primary purpose of marriage, the tradition also valued conjugal love for its own sake. The Hebrew Bible gives us the examples of Abraham, Jacob, and Elkanah, men who remain devoted to their wives, Sarah, Rebecca, and Hannah, despite many years of barrenness. In the book of Samuel, Elkanah tries to comfort his wife by saying, "Hannah, why do you weep? Why don't you eat? Why is your heart sad? Am not I better to you than ten sons?"[9]

Jewish law regulated marriage, but Jewish weddings reflected the dreams, tastes, and creative energy of Jews. Weddings repudiate past grief, celebrate the here and now, and affirm the promise of a joyful future. "Be fruitful and multiply" has been the cry of a people with a precarious place in the world. After the Holocaust it was said, "To dance at a Jewish wedding is to dance on Hitler's grave."

In Judaism's pantheon of folk characters, one of the most colorful is the *shadchan* (matchmaker). During the Middle Ages, matchmakers were learned men and rabbis, but by the eighteenth century they had become salespeople who glossed over physical defects and big discrepancies in age. But because the work of making marriages was considered so vital, the matchmaker's excesses were forgiven. According to a Yiddish proverb, "God does not punish the *shadchan* for telling lies." During the Enlightenment, when romantic love replaced the *shadchan* and couples made their own matches, there were dire warnings about the imminent demise of the Jewish people.

Marriage in the Twenty-First Century

Marriage is no longer the only way to fulfill financial, social, or sexual needs, nor is it the dividing line between childhood and adulthood. We marry and have children later than in the past, and remaining single is not the exception or the shame it used to be.

The twentieth and twenty-first centuries saw a radical redefinition of marriage, equalizing rights and protections for women and men and making it legal for same-sex couples in nations around the world. While these changes are not universal, much of the North American Jewish community has embraced them, with transformational results.

For example, the *ketubah*—a document originally meant to spell out the groom's fiduciary responsibilities to the bride—has been revised and rewritten in countless ways. *Kinyan*, the one-sided *halachic* transaction that enacts a marriage, has been reinterpreted, reinvented, and even replaced with the notion of *brit*, a sacred covenant.

The Faces under the Huppah
The wedding canopy is a showcase for far-reaching changes in the Jewish community, especially the full

inclusion of women in communal and religious life. In 1960, no one could have imagined brides wearing prayer shawls and *kippot*, much less serving as clergy and acting as witnesses. The sight of women under the *huppah* in all those roles—unimaginable for millennia—is now completely unremarkable.

Weddings today also shine a light on Judaism's embrace of diversity, a development with roots in the prophetic tradition. In the words of Isaiah: "Widen the place of your tent, stretch the curtains of your dwellings—stint not! Lengthen your cords and strengthen your stakes."[10]

The presence of converts to Judaism, of LGBTQ Jews, and of non-Jews under the *huppah* can be seen as a challenge—even a threat—to a tradition that has persevered by maintaining its boundaries. But the countervailing tradition of adaptability is the reason why Judaism has survived and thrived.

New faces under the *huppah* become part of the family; their relatives become extended family. Some worry that these additions will result in a watering down of Judaism and the Jewish people, but many others see it as a healthy infusion of living waters, *mayyim hayyim*, and another chapter in a long, lively, disputatious history.

Jews by Choice

While no reliable statistics are available for the number or rate of conversion to Judaism, it appears that more people have chosen to become Jewish during the past few generations than at any other time since the beginning

of the Common Era. The presence of new Jews is evident
everywhere, especially in commune leadership at all
levels.

Conversion to Judaism is largely a process of study,
usually directed by a rabbi, who sets the curriculum and
meets with candidates over months or years. In addition
to study, Jewish law requires *mikveh* (ritual immersion)
for men and women, and ritual circumcision for men.[11]
Converts also meet with a *bet din*, a rabbinical court,
usually three rabbis who question candidates about their
sincerity and knowledge of Judaism.

Since many converts find their way to Judaism as a result
of falling in love with a Jew, conversions and weddings
often take place within months or even weeks of each
other. While each of these life-changing transitions merits
recognition and celebration, the synergy adds another
layer of meaning.

Conversion to Judaism is also a choice made by about
one-third of the non-Jewish spouses married to Jews.[12]
When this happens, some couples decide to reaffirm
their marriage vows Jewishly: getting a *ketubah*, standing
beneath a *huppah*, and convening family and friends for a
celebration. These weddings can be intimate gatherings at
home or in a synagogue with only a few guests. However,
the weight of Jewish tradition is on the side of *simcha*,
which means "joy": in other words, guests, dancing, cake,
and gladness.

Jews by choice are Jews. Period. Any religious or liturgical distinction at a wedding would be inappropriate,

and it is up to individual Jews by choice to decide if they wish their conversion to be mentioned. In the past, pointing out a convert's non-Jewish history was considered an ethical breach, a way of challenging—and denigrating—their authenticity. Today, the decision to convert tends to be met with respect, admiration, and gratitude, and many are happy and proud to make it known.

Converts to Judaism can also choose how to honor and include non-Jewish family members and traditions in the wedding ceremony and celebration, with food, music, poetry, dance, forms of dress, and decoration.

Lesbian/Gay/Bisexual/Transgender/Queer Jews

Jewish values sometimes differ from those of the secular world; unfortunately the Jewish community shared the long history of ignoring, shunning, and doing harm to gays and lesbians.

In the 1980s, gay and lesbian Jews came out and demanded their rightful place at the communal table. The Reconstructionist movement began ordaining lesbian and gay rabbis in 1984, the Reform movement in 1990, the Conservative movement in 2006. Reform and Reconstructionist clergy officiated at gay weddings ("commitment ceremonies" prior to legalization) for more than a decade before the June 2015 US Supreme Court ruling that guaranteed same-sex couples the right to marry. Conservative rabbis now officiate at same-sex weddings as well. Orthodox denominations still do not, as of now, ordain or perform weddings for gay or lesbian Jews.

Now that same-sex wedding announcements in the *New York Times* or the temple bulletin are commonplace, gay weddings are no longer curiosities. LGBTQ Jewish couples face all the same wedding choices as straight couples. How traditional do we want our ceremony to be? Where do we find a compatible rabbi? What should we serve for dinner? Will we find a *ketubah* that speaks for us, or should we write our own?

For the most part, the task of finding a good rabbinic fit is essentially the same for all couples: you are looking for compatibility and comfort; for clergy who listen and want to help you create a healthy marriage as well as a beautiful wedding. (See page 19.) Any thoughtful rabbi will set up premarital counseling sessions about money, sex, resolving conflict, and creating a Jewish home, but clearly, rabbis who have married LGBTQ couples in the past have experience and sensitivity that can be especially helpful.

Rabbis with experience (whatever their sexual orientation) may be better prepared to provide guidance as you negotiate with families: How do we break the news of our wedding to Grandpa? Should we invite your fundamentalist-Christian uncle? My Orthodox cousins? They may be more aware of resources such as *ketubah* texts and blessing translations that have worked for other same-sex couples, gender-neutral liturgy, and biblical references to the relationship between Jonathan and David or Ruth and Naomi, and sensitivity to the brokenness of a world in which the vast majority of

LGBTQ people are not only unable to marry but are in fear for their lives.

Non-Jews under the Huppah

In an era when virtually all barriers between Jews and non-Jews are gone, intermarrying couples may be surprised by a cool, suspicious, or even hostile response to the announcement of an engagement. While there is no excuse for rudeness, it helps to understand how your marriage fits into the history of the Jewish people.

Until the late-twentieth century, marriage between a Jew and a non-Jew was nearly unthinkable and even dangerous. In some times and places, the church called it apostasy, a form of heresy punishable by death for both. For Jews, marriage to an outsider meant abandoning family, faith, and identity; when that happened, some parents would "sit *shiva*," mourning as if their child had died.

In 1965, intermarriage accounted for only 7 percent of Jewish weddings; by 2000, 30 to 50 percent of North American Jews were marrying non-Jews. Communal leaders— and parents—viewed that rate of change with alarm. Early studies that showed few children of intermarriage ultimately identified as Jews or affiliated with Jewish institutions led to dire predictions about the future.

Not all responses were negative; the Reconstructionist and Reform movements made concerted efforts to welcome non-Jewish spouses, and eventually to recognize the Jewishness of children born to Jewish fathers and non-Jewish mothers when given a Jewish education;* this opened doors to intermarried parents and welcomed a new generation of families.

In fact, intermarriage is the communal norm. Thanks to conversion as well as marriage between Jews and non-Jews, virtually every extended Jewish family now includes in-laws, cousins, nieces and nephews, uncles and aunts, who are Christian, Muslim, Buddhist, Hindu, or claim no religious affiliation.

Intermarrying couples seeking a Jewish wedding often come face-to-face with questions about religious belief and affiliation, about spirituality and blending families from different faith traditions, about how to answer when children ask about God or why Grandma goes to church and they go to temple.

A non-Jewish partner may wonder, Does my Catholicism (or Unitarianism) still mean anything to me? Why is my partner, who never does any anything Jewish, suddenly so adamant about having a Jewish ceremony? Why is this even a problem since I don't consider myself a member of any religion?

A Jewish partner may think, What *does* my Jewishness mean to me? Why do I care so much that a rabbi officiates? Am I doing this for my parents or for me?

Couples who can talk about religion before their weddings are much better prepared to handle knottier

---

*This is a departure from *halachah*, in which Jewish status is determined by the mother; if she is Jewish, so are her children, regardless of the father's religious identity.

questions later on. Sensitive clergy from one or both traditions are best equipped to help you sort through differences honestly and respectfully; some communities also run discussion groups to explore such issues.

Intermarrying couples tend to be painted with a single broad brush, but in fact, they are a diverse group who approach weddings with different hopes and expectations. For example, the term *interfaith* is only appropriate if the non-Jewish partner has an ongoing connection to another religion and wants that tradition reflected in the wedding ceremony and in married life. *Interfaith* does not apply to those who consider themselves "spiritual but not religious" or atheists, nor to those who are willing and even happy to have an unambiguously Jewish wedding and home.

In some cases, people who are religiously disconnected or unchurched are effectively "marrying in." These "Jews by affiliation" may not be ready for or interested in converting to Judaism, but will commit to supporting their partner's Jewish life and to provide any children they might have with a Jewish education and home life. Some who intermarry may eventually convert to Judaism, but many who do not take that step and share a Jewish life with their partners find themselves connected and committed and comfortably "Jew-ish."

For those who want a ceremony with an authentic connection to Jewish tradition, it is important to find a rabbi who can inform and guide your choices. It is no longer difficult to find clergy to perform a wedding between Jews and non-Jews; some rabbis and cantors require a commitment to establishing a Jewish home before meeting with couples; others have no such rules. What you want is a respectful and thoughtful partner in the joyful/sacred work of starting your married life together.

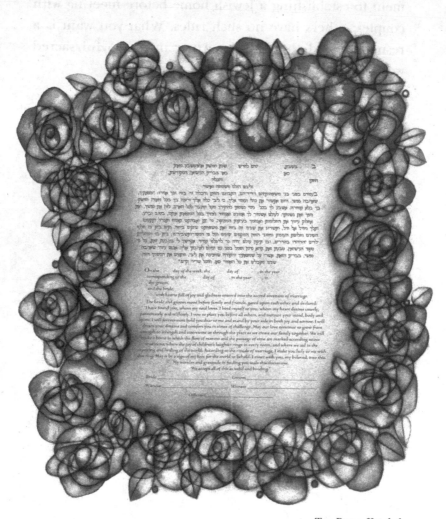

Two Dozen Ketubah
© Rachel Deitsch
www.newworldketubah.com

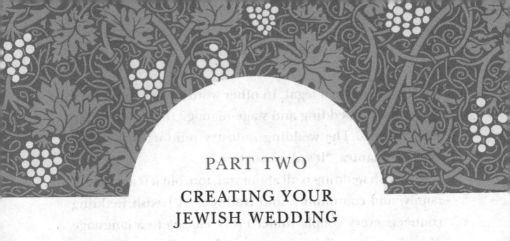

PART TWO

CREATING YOUR JEWISH WEDDING

Jewish life-cycle events function on several levels: personal, familial, communal, and temporal. A wedding is an announcement of love and commitment between two people. Weddings convene two families and knit them into one extended family. Every wedding creates a new household, which changes the fabric of the Jewish community forever. And all weddings connect couples to the history of lovers and marriages throughout time.

These considerations can get lost in the planning of a wedding. There are too many choices: rings, guest lists, seating charts. Planning a Jewish wedding adds even more choices: *ketubah, huppah, yichud.* Parents and friends will offer conflicting advice and examples, and the wedding industry stands ready to help, which means sell you things.

The Internet fosters an expectation of infinite choice and immediate gratification. It is possible to Google every question, write your own wedding script, hire a justice of the peace to officiate or have a friend or family member apply for online ordination or a temporary license from the state to make it legal. In other words, you can create a do-it-yourself wedding and stage-manage the whole thing, soup to nuts. The wedding industry reinforces this idea with the mantra, "It's all about you."

A Jewish wedding is all about you, too, but it is also about family, and community, and tradition. A Jewish wedding connects every couple under every *huppah* to a language of holiness, to a living history, and to a diverse and vital culture. A Jewish wedding places you at the center of a never-ending story—something much larger and more mysterious than two people.

Judaism sees every human being as a sacred creation, *b'tzelem Elohim*, made in the image of God. The Torah also says, "It is not good to be alone," which Judaism interprets with multilayered commitments: community is fundamental, the family table is an altar, teachers are essential, and marriage is a *mitzvah*.

To create a wedding that embraces all of these connections, it helps to have someone who can answer questions about ritual and custom and keep you focused on what matters, which is the love of your life. You need a knowledgeable guide to help you shape a meaningful celebration of your love and commitment. In other words, you need a rabbi. But not just any rabbi. You need to find *your* rabbi.

Finding Your Rabbi

The person who leads a Jewish wedding ceremony is called a *mesader kiddushin*, one who "orders" *kiddushin*, the ceremony of sanctification. While a *mesader kiddushin* does not have to be a member of the clergy, rabbis have fulfilled this role for a very long time; Maimonides, the twelfth-century authority, wrote that marriages required the supervision of an ordained rabbi.[1]

What happens under the *huppah* is only a small part of a rabbi's responsibilities as a wedding officiant. Rabbis are teachers (that's what *rabbi* means) who can explain the historical and communal framework of the wedding. Rabbis are professional ritualists with experience and resources to help create a memorable ceremony. Rabbis are counselors who can help you articulate hopes and dreams for your marriage and provide perspective and reassurance during the most joyful/stressful season of your life. Rabbis are acknowledged authority figures—which can be an important consideration for family members—who act on behalf of both the Jewish community and the secular state.

Cantors: As clergy, cantors also act as *mesader kiddu-shin*. Cantors are trained in Jewish liturgical music, which includes chanting from the Torah. Their primary responsibility is to lead congregational prayer and song, co-officiate at life-cycle events with a rabbi, and sometimes officiate on their own. Like a rabbi, a cantor—in Hebrew, *hazzan* (m) or *hazzanit* (f)—has the legal standing to sign secular marriage licenses. The discussion of the rabbi's role in this section applies to cantors who act as *mesader kiddushin*. And it may go without saying, but having a cantor under the *huppah*—either as officiant or co-officiant—adds the warmth and beauty of the human voice in song.

You might already know your rabbi: the beloved teacher of your childhood; your aunt who is a cantor; a friend who was recently ordained; the rabbi who guided you through conversion. Often, it's not so simple. Your hometown rabbi is not willing to perform a same-sex wedding or intermarriage. You don't know any rabbis and your last contact with one was at your bar mitzvah, which wasn't such a great experience.

Where to start? You can consult movement websites and online resources, some that address intermarrying and gay couples. (See "Resources.") If you are affiliated with a university, you are a de facto member of the campus Hillel congregation and you can approach the staff there. If you have friends who belong to a synagogue, or were married by a rabbi, ask them and other people you know and trust.

Once you have a name or two, attend a class or service the rabbi is leading and you'll probably know immediately whether or not you want to have a conversation with them.

Do not make assumptions based on a rabbi's age, gender, or affiliation; all rabbis make their own decisions about whom they will or won't marry, and how they run a service. Not every Reform rabbi will perform a marriage if one of the partners is not Jewish, and not all Conservative rabbis will refuse.

Once you have identified a likely candidate, make an appointment to meet; both members of the couple should attend. Only them. No parents. Bring questions. Ask the rabbi to describe the ceremony they usually perform and how open they are to making changes. Are they willing to include non-Jewish family members and friends in the wedding?

You should be specific and it's a good idea to bring up concerns and issues right off the bat. Are you worried about involving non-Jewish family members in the ceremony or how much of it will be in Hebrew? Is God referred to with masculine pronouns? How does the rabbi translate *Baruch ata Adonai*—a phrase that is repeated many times during a wedding?

This is a two-way interview, so be prepared to talk about yourselves: family history and religious background, edu-

cation, career, previous marriages, children, hopes for
your marriage. Rabbis may ask some surprising questions:
Why do you want to get married? Why now? What draws
you to celebrate your wedding with Jewish ritual? If either
of you have been married before, rabbis may ask about
that relationship and, if it was a Jewish marriage, may want
to know if there was a Jewish writ of divorce or *get*. (See
page 171.)

If you decide to work together, you can expect the rabbi
to initiate conversations about sensitive matters, from
money management to fighting fair to sex to envisioning
a Jewish life together. This can only happen in a relationship built on trust, so trust your gut.

Indeed, the only litmus test for making a match—a
shidduch—with a rabbi is your comfort level. After the first
meeting, ask yourselves, Did we feel free to ask questions?
Did the rabbi seem to understand our concerns? Did we
laugh? Did we learn something? Do we want to have coffee with this person? If the answer to these questions is yes,
you may have found your rabbi. If the answer is no, keep
looking.

It can be difficult to say no thanks to a rabbi who took
the time to meet and is willing to do the ceremony, but this
may be the most important decision you make in planning
your wedding. You are beginning a relationship, not con-
ducting a transaction. Besides, sometimes rabbis say no,
too; they have to feel comfortable and excited to work with
you. Saying no is not necessarily a judgment—it's about
chemistry.

But consider this: if you tell the rabbi that you've already picked the date and there's a nonrefundable deposit on the venue, you make it clear that the ceremony is something of an afterthought. Rabbis are not spiritual chauffeurs. It's important to communicate confidence in your ability to make Jewish decisions, but rabbis have limits and commitments that transcend your needs. You may make a request that crosses a line they cannot cross and remain true to their beliefs and religious practice. For example, some rabbis will not perform a ceremony until Shabbat has ended—sometimes an issue on long summer days. It is disrespectful, pointless, and self-defeating to insist on something a rabbi cannot, in conscience, go along with.

When all three of you agree it's a match, the rabbi will ask to meet a number of times before the wedding. Rabbis take seriously their role as premarital counselors. You may be asked to fill out questionnaires about family and past relationships, or to keep a journal in the months before the wedding.

Since your wedding is the beginning of a Jewish home, rabbis will inevitably want to talk about making your Jewish choices as a couple, including such topics as Shabbat and the yearly cycle of holidays, placing a *mezuzah* at the door, raising Jewish children, and becoming a member of the Jewish community.

Rabbis are often called upon to be peacemakers. As the Yiddish proverb says, "There is no *huppah* without crying." Clergy who have accompanied others down the rose-and-thorn-strewn path to the *huppah* can help you navigate the inevitable problems that arise as you're plan-ning the biggest party of your lives while melding two groups of strangers into one extended family. Even if you are respectful of each other's differences and have the most supportive parents imaginable, there will be stress. Every marriage is a blending of cultures, and whether you grew up in different religious traditions on opposite sides of the planet or both of you went to the same synagogue and Jewish summer camp, tension and tears are inevitable.

But when you and your beloved—or you and your mother—start yelling at each other about the order of the processional, you're not arguing about who's on first. Life-cycle events are emotionally charged turning points for the whole family, and your wedding may unearth old fears, family feuds, and stresses in the marriages around you.

Even minor misunderstandings and petty arguments deserve careful handling. Little things can get blown out of proportion and sour relationships for years. The more resolution and harmony you can achieve in the months prior to a wedding, the happier the wedding day for every-one, and with luck you will have set the stage for healthy family ties for the future. Rabbis are a great resource and sounding board as you navigate these waters.

Premarital meetings are more than simply appoint-ments to cross off a to-do list. These hours can be a wel-come pause in the hectic run-up to a wedding, time to take a breath, ponder the commitment you are making, and savor your love for each other. Finally, the relationship you create with your rabbi blossoms under the *huppah*, where the rabbi can speak about you with real understanding and talk to you with genuine fondness.

Remuneration

If you or your family belong to your rabbi's congregation, membership dues cover the clergy's services; however, it is both thoughtful and appropriate to make a donation to the rabbi's discretionary fund or other charity (*tzedakah*) in the rabbi's name. An honorarium is expected if you are not affiliated or if your rabbi does not serve a congregation. The amount should be discussed at your first meeting. If the cost would create a hardship, most rabbis will try to accommodate you. The honorarium and all expenses for travel, lodging, etc., should be paid promptly. If you invite your rabbi or cantor to the celebration after the wedding, be mindful of dietary needs: if the clergy or members of your wedding party keep kosher, platters of shrimp can be problematic.

WHO PAYS FOR WHAT?

Money is a common flash point. In the past, the rules were clear: the groom's family assumed all wedding costs since the bride's family was providing the dowry. More recently it's been customary for the bride's parents to assume the entire cost (a kind of latter-day dowry), except for such things as the groom's clothes and other incidentals, which become his family's responsibility.

The old paradigms have been shifting for years and same-sex marriage made all the rules moot. Since Jews tend to marry later, couples that have long been financially independent often prefer—and may be better able to afford—to pay their own wedding bills. It is also not uncommon for wedding costs to be shared two or three ways.

Regardless of how the costs of the wedding are divided, money is a potent symbol. Giving money can be a way of expressing love; a parent's refusal to pick up the tab for a child's wedding celebration can be a sign of disapproval. Likewise, refusing a parent's offer to pay can feel like rejection. Money also determines control. Whoever covers the costs generally—and reasonably—wants a say in the decision making. Though rabbis do not get involved in specifics, they can help you understand and address underlying issues.

One way to help minimize conflict about money and control is for the couple to prepare two lists. One is of non-negotiables—aspects of the wedding over which you are not prepared to compromise, which might include your *ketubah*, a no-rental-clothing rule, and a chocolate cake. The second list includes things about which you don't feel as strongly and are willing—maybe even happy—to hand over to someone else, such as flowers, location of the family dinner before the wedding, selecting accommodations for out-of-town guests.

Time and Place

*Jewish ritual may be characterized as the art of signifi-
cant forms in time, an architecture of time. Most of its
observances—the Sabbath, the New Moon, the festivals,
the Sabbatical, and the Jubilee year—depend on a certain
hour of the day or season of the year.*
—Abraham Joshua Heschel, *The Sabbath*[2]

When

There are almost no rules about *where* you can or can't
raise a *huppah. When*, however, is another matter. Fully one
out of every seven days—Shabbat—is off-limits.

Weddings are forbidden on Shabbat not only because
of the inevitable work and travel that would violate the
rules against working and making transactions on the
Sabbath, but also because of the injunction that every
simcha—every joy—be celebrated and savored individually. According to Jewish law, "one should not mix rejoicing with rejoicing." Combining the Sabbath and a wedding
means that one or both will not be given their due, which
is why double weddings are discouraged. As Rabbi Heschel
wrote, "Every hour is unique and the only one given at the
moment, exclusive and endlessly precious."[3]

Weddings are not held on major holidays and festivals,

including Rosh Hashanah, Yom Kippur, Passover, Shavuot, and Sukkot, but are permitted on Hanukkah and Purim. Traditionally, weddings do not take place on Tisha-b'Av, a day of public mourning for the destruction of the Temple, or on fast days (Gedaliah and Esther). Weddings are prohibited during the Omer, the seven weeks between Passover and Shavuot, with the exception of Lag b'Omer, a popular day for weddings in Israel.

Weddings are postponed for at least thirty days if either the bride or groom loses a parent, sibling, or child. But in general, the *mitzvah* of marriage is so important that weddings take precedence over almost everything else and in some cases may even preempt mourning. (If—God forbid—such a situation arises, your rabbi can advise you.)

Spring and fall weddings have been favored since biblical times. Springtime is celebrated in the Song of Songs (Shir haShirim), a collection of poems that read like wedding hymns: "The winter is past, the rain is over and gone; the flowers appear on the earth; the time of singing is come and the voice of the turtle is heard in our land." In ancient Israel, the fifteenth of Av—an autumn month—was a day unmarried girls would dress in white and go into the vineyards, where young men would go to seek brides.

Weddings were once carefully scheduled on days considered auspicious on the calendar, such as Rosh Hodesh, the new moon of the Jewish month when the moon begins to wax in the sky—a symbol of growth and fertility. Even the zodiac was consulted to invoke good spirits and fool evil ones.

Preference was also given to days of the week associated with good luck. Mondays were generally avoided because in the creation story, the phrase *and God saw how good this was* does not appear. Tuesday was favored because those words appear twice. The five-day workweek made Sunday the most popular day for Jewish weddings; Saturday-night weddings traditionally begin an hour and a half after sunset, to avoid overlapping with Shabbat. Today, the hour of the ceremony is a matter of personal choice, with evening weddings generally more formal than midday weddings.

Where
For Jews, any place can be made holy through intentions and actions, so a wedding can take place virtually anywhere. During the Middle Ages *huppot* were raised in cemeteries based on the belief that the life-affirming act of marriage could halt a plague.[4]

Although no descriptions of wedding ceremonies appear in the Bible, a *huppah* would doubtless have been raised outdoors. This custom carried over even after weddings moved into synagogues, where they were held in an outdoor courtyard. Outdoor weddings remain popular today, with *huppot* raised in arboretums, parks, rented estates, hotel lawns, beaches, family backyards, and synagogue courtyards—*always* with backup plans in place in case of bad weather.

Jewish weddings and celebrations are held in all kinds of venues: hotel ballrooms, historic homes, libraries, function halls, and, of course, synagogues.[5] A sanctuary offers a spirit of *kedusha*, holiness, and connects your wedding to the larger Jewish community. If your venue is a temple that one or both of you belong to or have visited or prayed in, the space itself can be a source of meaning.

In synagogues with complete kitchens and sizable function rooms, couples can hold the ceremony and the celebration under the same roof. In addition to the convenience, this allows you to carry the spirit of the wedding ceremony directly into the *simcha* that follows. It is also possible to have the *huppah* in a synagogue and move the celebration to another space.

Popular venues—including synagogues—are scheduled for months and even years in advance; book as soon as you can, especially if you have your heart set on a particular location in June or September.

Wherever you plan to wed, spend some time there as a couple, just the two of you. Imagine yourselves under a *huppah*, surrounded by family and friends. If you're marrying in a sanctuary, spend a few minutes there when it's empty and quiet. This, too, is part of planning a wedding, preparing you to savor the upcoming "endlessly precious" hour.

Invitations and Information

For most of Jewish history, weddings were not invitation-only events. In the *shtetels* of Eastern Europe and in Israeli *kibbutzim*, the whole community would consider itself invited because it was a *mitzvah* to rejoice with the bride and groom, who were known to everyone. This is still the case in some Israeli communities and some traditional congregations. For most couples, however, there is a guest list, which can be a source of conflict and even anguish.

The size of a guest list is determined by family obligations, budget, and the kind of celebration you want—intimate or expansive. The final tally is a composite of lists: the couple's and their respective parents'. It might seem fair to give the same number to each, but that doesn't work if, for example, there are thirty cousins on one side and only three on the other. Then there's the question of who gets priority: the couples' circle of friends or the parents' family friends. The result is always a compromise, so nobody is completely happy. Fortunately, Jewish tradition provides a whole round of gatherings so that many who don't attend the wedding still have a chance to celebrate with you. (See "Before the *Huppah*" on page 121.)

Until the mid-twentieth century, printed Jewish wedding invitations followed the dictates of secular etiquette; often the only indication that anything Jewish was going on was the location and perhaps a family name. Today, your choice of words can give guests a preview of the celebration, from the very first save-the-date e-mail. For example, instead of being "honored" to invite guests, you can be "delighted" to ask them to "dance at" your wedding rather than merely "attend." Using words such as *huppah* and *simcha* lets everyone know that you'll be honoring Jewish tradition, and if you're worried some of your guests won't understand, include translations.

You can also include the Hebrew date as well as the secular date:

June 20, which is the ** of Sivan 57**

or

** June 20**, which is 57** years after the creation of the world.

You can cite the Torah reading closest to your wedding date: *Sunday, August **, 20**—** of Av 57** following Shabbat Ekev.*

If your wedding falls on the first day of a Hebrew month—Rosh Hodesh, "the head of the month"—you can identify the date as *Sunday, June **, 20**—Rosh Hodesh Sivan 57**.*

As for location, you can invite guests to *the streets of Jerusalem, unless the Messiah tarries, in which case the wedding will be held at Temple Sinai.*

A few sample invitations follow:

On the [**] of Nissan, corresponding
to the [secular date]

[Beloved] and [Beloved]

Invite you to join them and their families

To rejoice as they celebrate their
love under the huppah

[Time and location]

Join us as we light the first candle of Hanukkah

and lead our children

[Beloved] and [Beloved] to the huppah

We will meet on [secular date/Hebrew date]

[Time and location]

[Parents] and [Parents]

Together with their parents

[Beloved] and [Beloved]

*Invite you to share in the joy and
celebration of their marriage*

on [date]

The ceremony begins at [time]

[Location]

[Parents] and [Parents]

Invite you to share in the joy of
their children's wedding

[Beloved] and [Beloved]

Will meet under the huppah

On [Hebrew date] which coincides
with [secular date]

[Location]

A line or two from the Song of Songs are sometimes featured on invitations: "I am my beloved's and my beloved is mine" and "This is my beloved, this is my friend." For outdoor weddings: "Come my beloved, let us go out to the field," or "You shall go forth in joy and in peace shall you be led. The mountains and hills shall burst into song before you, and all the trees of the field shall applaud. Like an apple tree among trees of the forest is my beloved among the youths" or "Like a rose among thorns is my darling among the maidens."

Another source for quotes is the seven wedding blessings: "You created joy and gladness, bride and groom [bride and bride, groom and groom, lover and friend], mirth and exultation, pleasure and delight."

You can also honor a family heritage with phrases written in Chinese or Hindi, Arabic or Spanish, Russian or Yiddish.

In keeping with the tradition of remembering the world's brokenness even during times of personal joy and celebration, some couples add a note requesting that guests bring canned goods to donate to a food pantry or make a donation to charity (see *tzedakah* on page 91):

Even as we celebrate this joyful occasion, we think of those in need, near and far. In lieu of a gift, we ask that you make a contribution to one of the following organizations or to a charity of your choice.

Design

Invitations are a canvas for creativity and *hiddur mitzvah*, the rabbinic mandate for the beautification of Jewish life. Familiar icons such as six-pointed stars, pomegranates, and wedding canopies connect you to Jewish tradition, but you can also use images that reflect your interests and passions: the natural world, animals, travel.

Some couples send engraved invitations on beautiful card stock (which should be mailed at least six weeks in advance of the wedding), but some invitations, and many announcements, RSVPs, and other enclosures, have migrated to the Web. Wedding websites make it easy to communicate directions to venues, hotel recommendations, gift registries, and more. Websites also give you room to explain the details of your Jewish wedding, from a glossary of Hebrew and Yiddish words, to descriptions of the ceremony and celebration.

In addition to information on the wedding website, some couples create a printed guide to hand out on the day of the ceremony. This can be a simple glossary or a small booklet with words of welcome, a brief description of the ceremony, or a guide to the liturgy. Some booklets also include the *ketubah* text, the seven wedding blessings, English readings, and the text of *birkat hamazon*, the blessings that conclude the celebration.

Clothes and Rings

*God has dressed me with garments of exultation . . . as
a bridegroom puts on a priestly diadem, and as a bride
adorns herself with her jewels.*

—Isaiah 61:10

While priestly diadems have been out of fashion for
millennia, wedding attire and adornment remain important, and not just an exercise in vanity. These are the most
important—and most photographed—clothes most of
us will ever own. The Talmud warned against excessive
displays of finery that might embarrass poor relatives, still
a worthy consideration, and modesty (variously defined)
is encouraged. But even a quick historical survey of
paintings, drawings, and descriptions of Jewish wedding
clothes demonstrates how Jews have copied local fashion.
In Europe, brides started wearing long white gowns and
long trains after their Christian neighbors did; in North
Africa and the Middle East, Jewish brides donned bright
colors and veils decorated with gold coins. Grooms' clothing mirrored the contemporary men's fashions as well.

Veils have been part of bridal dress through the ages,
hearkening back to the biblical Rebecca, who "took a veil
and covered herself" when she first saw Isaac, her husband-

39

to-be. According to Jewish folklore, the veil gives the bride "special eyes" with which to watch over her children and grandchildren until the end of generations.

Some brides say that a veil is the one item of clothing that makes them feel set apart and uniquely "bridal"; for others, veils are irredeemably connected to women's oppression and dispense with them entirely. Some women put on a special *kippah*; others wear a hat or fascinator as a nod to—or a wink at—tradition.

The wearing of white at a Jewish wedding has more to do with spiritual purity than physical virginity. A white dress indicated that the bride had been to the *mikveh*, the ritual bath, and was ready for the wedding night. Because a wedding is considered a personal day of repentance and forgiveness, some grooms wear a *kittel*, a short white robe, over their clothes. A *kittel* is worn on Yom Kippur, at Passover seders, and as a burial shroud. However, this is not the custom in Sephardic communities, where grooms sometimes wrap themselves and their brides in a large prayer shawl, creating an intimate —often-white—*huppah* beneath the *huppah*.

For couples that wish to avoid gendered modes of dress, both can wear a *kittel* (available online and at Judaica stores), or dress each other in new prayer shawls or yarmulkes. One couple used their *tallisim* as "veils," covering themselves and then revealing their faces to see each other "as we are, without pretense."[6]

Because the *mitzvah*/obligation of rejoicing at a wedding is incumbent upon the couple as well as the guests, choose clothes that make you feel fabulous and avoid anything that might get in the way of your enjoyment—including a tight waist or uncomfortable shoes. Whatever you wear should make you feel attractive *and* ready to dance the night away.

Rings

Rings are a universal symbol of perfection, completion, unity, and the female. The mystics who wrote the Zohar saw the ring as a circle of light representing the sexual mystery of marriage.[7] For wedding couples, rings are visible tokens of love and fidelity, and hope for an unbroken union. In a Jewish wedding, the giving of a ring is a legal transaction as well as a romantic symbol.

Traditional Jewish law and customs about the kind of ring to be used are concerned with its legal function. Rings were to be free of precious stones, so that the value could not be misrepresented—the same reason wedding bands were to be made of a single metal, with no holes, gaps, or embellishments. However, Jews have long observed this mandate in the breach, with embellishments of every kind, especially engraved words: *mazel tov* (good luck), the couple's Hebrew names, the date of their wedding, and phrases such as *Ani Dodi v'Dodi Li* ("I am my beloved's and my beloved is mine"). The large, ornate rings of medieval weddings—big as a golf ball and often decorated with a castle—were owned by the community and loaned for ceremonial use only.

בשני בשבת בעשרים ושמונה יום לחודש שבט שנת חמשת אלפים ושבע מאות
ושש ושישים ושמונה למנין שאנו מונין כאן באאפר ניאק ניו יורק אמריקה הצפונית, בכוננות
עשרתם וחכמים. גם אברהם בן יציק ורחל ושרה בת נפתלי ולאה הגאהלכם
תחת חופת ונישואין. עם שאנו לדרכינו המשותפת, אנו מבטיחים לאהוב,
לחקור. לבר ולהנשא זה את זה. לבבותינו מתערים יחדיו לברוא עולם יחודינו
שמבוסרה חבריות, חבנה והחדנות. באוחדותו זה אנו שותפיכם לחקיר ולתמוך
אשר כרשהו ולגלות רגישות לצרכינו. משפה זה את זה ברצעו, רוחנים ותכונה,
מודעים תמיד חרושי לכל חודך נחשעות לשקידד ולהתמשיך בשאיפותינו. אנו
ושאבתם האחך חרדושי לכל חודך נחשעות לשקיד ולהתמיך בשאיפותינו. יושר
עבצחים לחגוב את השמחות בחינוי טוך ולהתגבר על הקשיים בנחישות
והחלשות. כי ייקן ונשבר לשבר את החינוך והתום המעטרדים אמן, יושר
וותקשורת. משותפים לחיים, נתאר לבנית בית תבוקרין כזה, זה, כמו האמרה
סבלמות ותריקה. מחבשמיו זה בעיניו על זה, בגלה עולם חדש ויתקיים כמו האמרה
"טובים השנים מן האחד." והכל שדיר וקיים:

*O*n the second day of the week, the twenty-eighth day of the month
of Shevat in the year 5768, corresponding to the fourth day of
February in the year 2008 here in Upper Nyack, New York, USA,
in the presence of family and friends, the beloveds Abe Franklin,
son of Sylvia and Frank Franklin, and Sarah Freedman, daughter
of Norman and Leah Freedman, entered into the covenant
of marriage.

As we embark on life's journey, we promise to love, cherish,
encourage and inspire one another. Our hearts fuse together,
creating a unique bond with friendship and compassion at its
core. Through this union, we vow to value and support each other,
always striving to show sensitivity to each other's needs. We shall
nurture one another emotionally, spiritually and intellectually,
always mindful of our respective qualities and strengths.
May we continue to grow together, maintaining the courage and
determination to pursue our desired paths. We promise to celebrate
life's joys with grace and overcome life's adversities with tenacity.
May we maintain the intimacy that fosters trust, honesty and
communication. As life partners, we shall strive to build a home
emanating love, peace, tolerance and charity. Through each other's
eyes, we see the world anew: may we be better together. All this is
valid and binding.

Witness _____ עד
Witness _____ עד
Rabbi _____ הרב
Bride _____ הכלה
Groom _____ החתן

Persian Arch Kaleidoscope Ketubah
© Diane Sidenberg
Image courtesy of www.ketubbah.com

Your *Ketubah*

The Midrash described the Torah as a *ketubah*—a marriage contract—between God and the people of Israel. The Jewish marriage contract, the *ketubah* (Hebrew for "written thing"), dates back to the end of the first century CE, when it was written in Aramaic, the language of Talmudic law, rather than Hebrew, the language of the Song of Songs.

Infinity of Love Ketubah
© Michelle Rummel
Image courtesy of www.ketubah.com

A traditional *ketubah* does not mention love or the establishment of a Jewish home or God. It is not a contract between the couple; they do not even sign it. The signatories are witnesses who testify that the groom "acquired" the bride in the prescribed manner, that he agreed to support her and set out terms for divorce, and that she entered into the marriage of her own free will and as a virgin. Historically, the witnesses were two observant Jewish men who had no family ties to either bride or groom. However, for generations rabbis and cantors, or other community leaders, signed.

The *ketubah* was then given to the bride as a guarantee of her rights and her husband's duties, and it became her (not their) possession. The document used in Orthodox circles today remains very much the same as *ketubot* written in the second century CE. (See the *ketubah* on page 183.) Although it seems antiquated and patriarchal to modern eyes, it was progressive for its time in providing women with legal status and rights in marriage, and because it made divorce a more costly decision, it was credited with strengthening the Jewish family.

Although a *ketubah* was not required—the ring, the *haray aht*, and two witnesses sufficed—without it the union of husband and wife was considered "unhallowed cohabitation." For example, in 1306, when Jews were stripped of their belongings and expelled from France, the rabbinic authorities declared that until new *ketubot* were delivered to the wives, there could be no conjugal relations.[8]

Exceptions were always allowed. *Ketubot* were sometimes lost or destroyed, and if witnesses testified that a Jewish couple were living together as husband and wife, a *bet din*, a court of rabbis, could rule that a *ketubah* was in effect.

Although the essence of the *ketubah* did not change, additions were made to meet current needs, as when they included pledges by the groom not to take "adventurous voyages or to expose himself to the risks of travellers and traders."[9] Sephardic *ketubot* sometimes embellished names with long lists of honorifics: ". . . the bridegroom, who bears the good, resplendent name, the perspicacious, the wise, of holy seed, the honorable Abraham, a pure Sephardi, the son of the honorable, who bears a good name, the exalted gentleman, the uplifted one in name and praise, the wise and perspicacious one, of holy seed, the honored Rabbi and teacher . . ."[10]

A traditional *ketubah* includes a statement that the document should not be regarded as an *ashakhta*, "a mere formula," but as early as the nineteenth century, the Reform movement rejected its use for that very reason, deeming it archaic and insulting to women. Among liberal Jews for much of the twentieth century, *ketubot* were either not used at all or were a vestigial practice, with a printed form provided by the rabbi.

This changed during the 1970s, when liberal Jews reclaimed and in some cases reinvented many rituals and traditions that had become "mere formula." The *ketubah* became a thoughtful expression of commitment and love as clergy and calligraphers added to or rewrote old texts and also created brand-new ones. Artists used every style and medium to make them beautiful.

Today, selecting a *ketubah* is a standard part of Jewish wedding preparations. Given the number of options for text, language, decoration, and witnesses, your *ketubah* can reflect your values, the way you see yourselves spiritually and religiously, and your taste in art.

Text

Ketubah websites and artist/calligrapher sites offer hundreds of options: Traditional Orthodox, Sephardic Orthodox, Reform, Conservative, biblically infused, secular humanist, interfaith. Many use egalitarian language that works for heterosexual couples, intermarrying couples, and same-sex couples. Many *ketubah* websites and artists will modify texts to your specifications.

An Orthodox *ketubah* is, by definition, complete and binding. However, no rule prohibits additions, which can be a list of mutual responsibilities, promises, and dreams for the marriage. Many now add a codicil requiring a civil and a religious divorce (*get*) in case the marriage ends, such as the Conservative movement's Lieberman clause (see page 60).

Language

Orthodox *ketubot* are written in Aramaic, its original language, but most couples opt for Hebrew with an English translation. Translations from Hebrew can be faithful to the original or you can choose an entirely different statement of love and commitment. English-only texts are also available, and if either or both of you speak another language—Spanish, Russian, Japanese, Hindi, Yiddish—you can include phrases or paragraphs in the English version, or opt for two translations of the Hebrew.

Witnesses

Jewish law requires that a *ketubah* be witnessed and signed by two observant Jewish men. However, since there is no rule against making additions to the document, some traditional *ketubot* have space for more signatories.

Contemporary *ketubot* are typically signed by the two beloveds, the rabbi, and two or more witnesses who are asked to take an active role not only in the wedding but as a source of emotional support to the couple in their marriage.

The *ketubah* is signed before the wedding ceremony—sometimes privately, and sometimes in front of the entire company. After the wedding, some couples invite all of their guests to sign on a large mat around the *ketubah* and/or display their *ketubah* on an easel during the celebration.

Decoration

The *ketubah* has a long and glorious history of embellishment. The earliest-known decorated *ketubah* date from the tenth century. The Jews of Persia made *ketubot* that seem to float on magic Oriental carpets, and North African Jews surrounded the text with intricate geometrical shapes similar to those that adorned the mosques of their Muslim neighbors. The Italian *ketubot* of the seventeenth and eighteenth centuries are alive with birds, flowers, signs of the zodiac, representations of biblical lovers, and even pagan gods and goddesses.

While a simple text meticulously lettered on fine paper can be timeless and elegant, color and design transform a contract into a work of art. Modern *ketubah* artists employ techniques ranging from paper cutting to lithography, silk-screening to watercolor, in a wide range of prices. An Internet search for *ketubah* will yield thousands of links to individual artists and sites that represent many artists.

Most *ketubot* are high-quality reproductions, some in limited editions. Calligraphers also create made-to-order *ketubot*, which require several months' notice. For those with the time and inclination, it is considered a great *mitzvah* to write and decorate your own *ketubah*.

After the Wedding

According to Jewish law, the *ketubah* becomes the property of the bride. In Persia, women kept them in a silk envelope under their pillows. Today, *ketubot* are jointly owned and often framed and displayed at home. If you shared the same bed before your wedding, hanging a *ketubah* over it affirms the change in your relationship.

The Baal Shem Tov, the founder of Hasidism, said that if a couple were fighting, they should read the *ketubah* aloud to remind each other of their wedding day, when they were surrounded with love and good wishes, and when God entered their relationship.[11]

Celtic Lion of Judah Ketubah
© Ginny Reel
www.ketubah-arts.com

KETUBAH TEXTS

ALTERNATIVE EGALITARIAN KETUBAH

On the ___ day of the week, the __ day of the month of
_____, in the year 57__, corresponding to the __
day of _____ in the year 20___ here in _____,
the beloveds, _____ and _____, entered into
this mutual covenant as equal partners, loving and supportive companions in life.

These rings symbolize our commitment to each other
as beloveds and friends before God and these witnesses.
We shall treasure and respect each other with honor and
integrity as we create a loving future together. May our
love provide us with the determination to be ourselves
and the courage to pursue our chosen paths. With this
ceremony we affirm our intention to provide for each
other the protections and privileges of all loving couples.
May our lives be intertwined forever and be as one in
tenderness and devotion.

As we share life's everyday experiences, we promise
to strive for an intimacy that will enable us to express
our innermost thoughts and feelings; to be sensitive at
all times to each other's needs; to share life's joys and to
comfort each other through life's sorrows; to challenge
each other to achieve intellectual and physical fulfillment
as well as spiritual and emotional tranquility.

We also promise to establish a home amid the community of Israel, committed to the creation of an

all-inclusive society; a loving environment dedicated to peace, hope and respect for all people; a household filled with love and learning, goodness and generosity, comfort and compassion.

We joyfully enter into this covenant and solemnly accept its obligations. All this is valid and binding.

—© MICKIE CASPI AND CASPI CARDS & ART

WWW.CASPICARDS.COM

BRIT KIDDUSHIN

At this time, the ___ day of _____ 57__, corresponding to the ___ day of ___ 20___, we, _____ and _____, celebrate in public our choice of each other as loving partners. We promise to love, respect, and support each other. We hope to sustain each other in a life of peace and fulfillment. We therefore pledge:

To share our lives together in joy and hardship, the everyday and the special moments; to contribute to each other's personal and emotional growth; to open ourselves to each other in trust; to be partners in decision-making, family roles, and in child-rearing, should we be so blessed; to consider each other's feelings and to settle our differences through self-examination, dialogue, and compromise.

We thereby hope to become one in body and one in spirit while yet becoming more fully individual selves. And we thereby declare our intention to become a true family among the families of Israel: to have a reverence for the sacred; to sanctify our lives in Torah; to maintain consciousness of the mysteries of life; to live with reverence and compassion for all people; and to open our home to those in need.

—RABBI EDWARD FELD

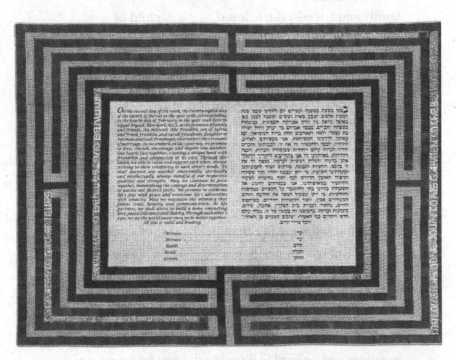

Song of Songs Labyrinth Ketubah
© Temma Gentles
Image courtesy of www.ketubah.com

MYSTICAL *KETUBAH*

On the ___ day of the week, the ___ day of the month of ___, in the year 57__, corresponding to the ___ day of the month of _____, in the year 20__, here, in the presence of family and friends, the beloved, _____, child of _____ and _____, and the beloved, _____, child of _____ and _____, have entered the covenant of marriage.

The sages tell us that when the world was created, everything fit perfectly like the pieces in a puzzle. There was beauty; there was peace; there was love. Over time, the pieces were blown apart and scattered.

But every time two souls come together in love and harmony, the puzzle comes together a bit more. The light of their joining is greater than the light they cast alone.

As we set out on our journey, we know there will be pockets of darkness. May we have the courage to pass through. Let us honor our separateness but know that together our light is a beacon to show us our way.

May our light shine back upon the traditions of our ancestors and forward to illumine the way for future generations.

Let our love shine a light to repair the world.

May we be better in being together.

—© JENNIFER RAICHMAN,
WWW.JENNIFERRAICHMAN.COM

I am my beloved's and my beloved is mine

אני לדודי ודודי לי

ביום א', כ"ג בחודש שבט, שנת חמשת אלפים שבע מאות שבעים ושבע, בג'קסונוויל, פלורידה, דנה ומלך באו בברית הנישואין כאוהבים חברים לחיים. כאוהבים וחברים אנו בוחרים ללכת יחדיו בשביל החיים. אנו מבטיחים להיות שותפים שווים, חברים נאמנים, ולתמוך אחד בשני במשך כל חיינו. חיינו כעת שזורים יחדיו לנצח. הדומה יחבר אותנו יחדיו, השונה ישאיר אותנו עוד, ואהבתנו תגדיר אותנו. נשתף את תקוותינו וחלומותינו ונחגוג יחד את כל מעברי החיים בשמחה ובאות כבוד. בעתות שמחה נוקיר זה את זו, ובעתות מצוקה נגן זה על זו. אנו מתחייבים להקים בית מלא צחוק, חמלה, אמונה, אמונה, כבוד ואהבה. בית המכיל כבוד למסורת אותה ירשנו, ושירוי וחובה למורשת משפחותינו. שנזכה כל יום ביום הראשון שלנו יחדיו. מוקפים בבני משפחה וחברים, אנו באים ברצון בברית זו של ידידות ואהבה מיום זה ואילך, אנו נהיה אחד.

ON THE NINETEENTH DAY OF THE MONTH OF FEBRUARY, IN THE YEAR TWO THOUSAND SEVENTEEN, HERE IN JACKSONVILLE, FLORIDA, DANA GREENBERG AND ADAM RAICHMAN ENTER THE COVENANT OF MARRIAGE AS LOVING COMPANIONS IN LIFE. AS BELOVEDS AND FRIENDS WE CHOOSE TO WALK LIFE'S PATH TOGETHER. WE PLEDGE TO BE EQUAL PARTNERS, LOVING FRIENDS, AND SUPPORTIVE COMPANIONS ALL THROUGH OUR LIFE. OUR LIVES ARE NOW FOREVER INTERTWINED. OUR SIMILARITIES WILL BIND US, OUR DIFFERENCES WILL ENRICH US, AND OUR LOVE WILL DEFINE US. WE WILL SHARE OUR HOPES AND DREAMS, AND CELEBRATE ALL OF THE PASSAGES OF LIFE TOGETHER WITH JOY AND REVERENCE. IN TIMES OF HAPPINESS WE WILL CHERISH EACH OTHER, AND IN TIMES OF TROUBLE WE WILL PROTECT EACH OTHER. WE WILL BUILD A HOME TOGETHER AND FILL IT WITH LAUGHTER, EMPATHY, FAITH, TRUST, FRIENDSHIP, COMPANIONSHIP AND LOVE; A HOME IN WHICH HOLIDAYS AND HERITAGE ARE CELEBRATED IN ACCORDANCE WITH OUR TRADITIONS. MAY WE LIVE EACH DAY AS THE FIRST, THE LAST, THE ONLY DAY WE WILL HAVE WITH EACH OTHER. SURROUNDED BY FAMILY AND FRIENDS, WE JOYFULLY ENTER INTO THIS COVENANT OF COMPANIONSHIP AND LOVE. FROM THIS DAY FORWARD, WE ARE AS ONE.

WITNESS _____ עד   WITNESS _____ עד

BRIDE _____ כלה   GROOM _____ חתן

RABBI _____ רב

Green Laurel Ketubah
© Jennifer Raichman
www.jenniferraichman.com

BRIT AHUVIM, LOVERS' COVENANT[12]

This document, created by Professor Rachel Adler, was written to replace the *ketubah*, which is based on *kinyan*, a legal instrument that enables the acquisition of one partner by another. For an explanation and the *brit ahuvim* ceremony, see page 147.

On ___ [day of the week], the ___ [day] of _____ [month], 57__, according to Jewish reckoning, ___ [month] ___ [day], ___ [year], according to secular reckoning in the city of _____, _____ [state], _____ [nation], _____ [Hebrew name], daughter/son of _____ and _____ whose surname is _____, and _____ [Hebrew name], daughter/son of _____ and _____ whose surname is _____, confirm in the presence of witnesses a lovers' covenant between them and declare a partnership to establish a household among the people of Israel.

The agreement into which _____ and _____ are entering is a holy covenant like the ancient covenants of our people, made in faithfulness and peace to stand forever. It is a covenant of protection and hope like the covenant God swore to Noah and his descendants, saying, "When the bow is in the clouds, I will see it and remember the ever-lasting covenant between God and all living creatures, all flesh that is on earth. That," God said to Noah, "shall be the sign of the covenant that I have established between me and all flesh." (Genesis 9:16–17)

It is a covenant of distinction, like the covenant God made with Israel, saying, "You shall be My people, I shall be your God." (Jeremiah 30:22)

It is a covenant of devotion, joining hearts like the covenant David and Jonathan made, as it is said, "And Jonathan's soul was bound up with the soul of David. Jonathan made a covenant with David because he loved him as himself." (1 Samuel 18:1)

It is a covenant of mutual loving-kindness like the wedding covenant between God and Zion, as it is said, "I will espouse you forever. I will espouse you with righteousness and justice and loving-kindness and compassion. I will espouse you in faithfulness and you shall know God." (Hosea 2:19–20)

PROVISIONS OF THE COVENANT:

The following are the provisions of the lovers' covenant in which _____ [Hebrew name], daughter/son of _____ and _____, and _____ [Hebrew name], daughter/son of _____ and _____, now enter:

1. _____ and _____ declare that they have chosen each other as companions as our rabbis teach: "Get yourself a companion. This teaches that a person should get a companion, to eat with, to drink with, to study Bible with, to study Mishnah with, to sleep with, to confide all one's secrets, secrets of Torah and secrets of worldly things." (Avot D'Rabbi Natan 8)

2. _____ and _____ declare that they are set-

ting themselves apart for each other and will take no
other lover.

3. _____ and _____ hereby assume all the
rights and obligations that apply to family members:
to attend, care, and provide for one another (and for
any children with which they may be blessed) (and
for _____, _____, and _____, child/children of
_____).

4. _____ and _____ commit themselves to a
life of kindness and righteousness as a Jewish family and
to work together toward the communal task of mend-
ing the world.

5. _____ and _____ pledge that one will help
the other at the time of dying, by carrying out the last
rational request of the dying partner, protecting him/
her from indignity or abandonment, and by tender faithful presence with the beloved until the end, fulfilling
what has been written: "Set me as seal upon your arm,
for love is stronger than death." (Song of Songs 8:6)

EGALITARIAN *KETUBAH* (CONSERVATIVE) WITH LIEBERMAN CLAUSE*

On the _____ day of the week, the _____ day of the month _____, in the year 57__, as we are accustomed to reckon it here, in _____ in the United States of America, we hereby testify that the groom _____ of the family _____ said to the bride _____ of family _____, "You are consecrated to me as my wife, with this ring, according to the laws of Moses and Israel," and that the bride _____ said to the groom _____, "You are consecrated to me as my husband with this ring, according to the laws of Moses and Israel." The groom _____ and the bride _____ accepted all the conditions of betrothal and marriage as set forth by biblical law and by the rulings of the Sages of blessed memory. The groom and bride further agreed willingly to work for one another, to honor, support, and nurture one another, to live with one another, and to build together a household of integrity as befits members of the Jewish people. The bride accepted a ring from the groom, and the groom accepted a ring from the bride, for the purposes of creating this marriage and to symbolize their love. The groom and bride also accepted full legal responsibility for the obligations herein taken on,

---

*The Lieberman clause, named for its author, Rabbi Saul Lieberman, was affirmed by the Conservative movement Joint Law Conference. Conservative rabbis generally require its addition to the *ketubot* of couples they marry.

as well as for the various property entering the marriage from their respective homes and families, and agreed that the obligations in this *Ketubah* may be satisfied even from movable property. We have had both the groom and the bride formally acquire these obligations to the other, with an instrument fit for such purposes. Thus all is in order and in force.

—RABBI GORDON TUCKER

And both together agreed that if this marriage shall ever be dissolved under civil law, then either husband or wife may invoke the authority of the Beth Din of the Rabbinical Assembly and the Jewish Theological Seminary of America or its duly authorized representatives, to decide what action by either spouse is then appropriate under Jewish matrimonial law; and if either spouse shall fail to honor the demand of the other to carry out the decision of the Beth Din or its representative, then the other spouse may invoke any and all remedies available in civil law and equity to enforce compliance with the Beth Din's decision and this solemn obligation. (Lieberman clause)

Your *Huppah*

The bridal canopy is a multifaceted symbol: it is a home, a garment, and a bedcovering. Its openness recalls the tent of the biblical Abraham, a paragon of hospitality, who kept his tents open on all sides so that visitors would know they were welcome. The tabernacle built in the desert to house the presence of God is described as a bridal canopy. According to Midrash, God created ten splendid *huppot* for the marriage of Adam and Eve.

The *huppah* is a symbol of God's presence at a wedding and in the home being established under the canopy. It was said the divine Name hovers above it, sanctifying the space below; after the ceremony, some rabbis invite couples to stand inside to recall—or anticipate—their own weddings.

Starting in the sixteenth century, probably in Poland, a portable canopy held aloft by four poles came into use. In some European communities, the embroidered Torah ark coverings (*parochet*) were used as the covering, but over time it became the custom to marry under a *tallis*, which was frequently a gift from the bride's family to the groom. The *tzitzit* (ritual fringes) on the prayer shawl hanging above the couple's heads were a reminder of the *mitzvot* they represent and regarded as a talisman against evil spirits. According to *gematria*, a numerical system in which every Hebrew letter has a number value, the thirty-two bunches of *tzitzit* correspond to the letters in the word *lev*, which means "heart."

The only rule about the construction of a *huppah* is that it be a temporary structure made by human hands. Other than that, it's yours to create.

Most synagogues and some caterers own *huppot*, which they loan to marrying couples; often, these are made to fit on a stationary frame. These kinds of *huppah* covers might be embroidered, quilted, or woven and decorated with familiar Jewish icons such as *kiddush* cups, Stars of David, scenes of Jerusalem, and text and images from the seven marriage blessings. Heavenly bodies represent the hope for future generations as numerous as the stars in the heavens.

The use of a large prayer shawl is still a popular choice and affirms a commitment to a shared Jewish life. Using a grandparent's *tallis* or a family-heirloom lace tablecloth connects your past and your future and makes for a good story to share with your guests. Because any fabric can serve, *huppot* can celebrate diverse family cultures with an Indian sari, Scottish tartan, lace mantilla, African textile, or Native American blanket.

Making your own *huppah* is a *mitzvah*; the gift of one is priceless. *Huppot* have been created with batik, silk screen, embroidery and needlepoint, woven wool, a cat's cradle of ribbons. An elaborate pieced-quilt *huppah* can become a family treasure, as can a linen cloth with children's handprints stamped in fabric paint.

When a *huppah* is handheld, it can be used in the processional, carried by four friends or relatives who also hold it aloft during the ceremony and represent the community that will support you in years to come.

Huppah poles should be long enough to stand on the ground and can be made of any material; wooden dowels can be cut to length; bamboo is both lightweight and handsome. According to ancient custom, on the birth of a daughter parents would plant a cedar tree, on the birth of a son a cypress, in anticipation of harvesting their branches for a *huppah*. Poles can be carved, painted, or wrapped in ribbons or flowers and greenery. The sky is the limit on creativity: one couple fastened their *huppah* over brightly colored helium balloons.

After the wedding, a *huppah* can become a wall hanging or a bedspread. Some couples loan theirs for weddings of family and friends, and some have raised their *huppah* for a baby-naming or *brit* ceremony.

THE SUCCAH AND THE HUPPAH

We live in the world; most of us live in houses
and apartment buildings, near busy streets.
But there are two temporary structures that
we build in our lifetimes. One is the succah,
the desert booth. The other is the huppah, the
wedding canopy.

Every year, the succah reminds us that once we
had no permanent place, no land where we
could sow and expect to reap at the end of a
long growing season. It reminds us that once
we were wanderers in the wilderness, and we
longed for a home. We talk about how easily
the succah collapses. It has firm walls, so that
we can almost pretend that it is real, but we lay
tree branches across the roof for thatch, tie
paper birds and gourds from the rafters, and
count the stars through the leaves.

The huppah is different. Who could mistake
it for a real house? Its walls are nonexistent.
The roof is flimsy. Wind can blow through the
huppah. The rain is welcome. The couple who

stand under its shelter must leave it to look up
and see the stars.

But it is the huppah that we take for our home
when we are promising each other everything.
It is raised, for most of us, once in a lifetime.
It is not permanent. But it is the promise of a
home.

Its openness pledges that there will be no secrets.
Friends and family stand at the corners,
weighing the fragile structure down. The roof
is often a tallis so that the bride and groom*
are covered by holiness and the memory of
commandments.

The huppah does not promise that love or
hope or pledges will keep out weather or
catastrophe. But its few lines are a sketch for
what might be.

The bridal couple* have left the desert of their
loneliness. They have come from far away to
be together. The flimsiness of the huppah
reminds them that the only thing that is real

---

*The poet invites you to substitute the word "beloveds."

about a home is the people in it who love and choose to be together, to be a family. The only anchor that they will have will be holding on to each other's hands.

The huppah is the house of promises. It is the home of hope.

—© DEBRA CASH, USED WITH PERMISSION

Witnesses and Guests

A marriage can be valid without a rabbi but not without witnesses. The Hebrew word for "witness," *ayd*, shares a common root with the word *od*, meaning "duration"; witnesses give permanence to human actions.[13] All of your guests will see you marry, but those we designate witnesses formally accept the responsibility for validating it; they also promise to be present in years to come, a responsibility that lasts "for one hundred and twenty years," the biblical life span of Moses.

At the beginning of the ceremony, the rabbi may introduce the witnesses, explain their role, and ask if they accept the obligations involved. Witnesses stand where they can see and hear the couple, and where the couple can see them.

Traditionally, the two witnesses must be observant Jewish men who are not related to each other or to the bride or groom. *Observant* in this context means obeying the laws regarding Shabbat, keeping kosher, and being mindful of the Torah's commandments. A person who is considered observant by some will be a heretic to others, so to avoid discord it became customary for the rabbi and the cantor or other community leader to serve as witnesses.

Jewish law exempts women from serving as witnesses

and other "time-bound" responsibilities, including communal worship. Often explained as an example of the Talmud's respect for women's primary duties as mothers and wives, these exemptions prevented them from taking part in the public life of the community.

Today, women routinely act as witnesses. Even when fulfilling the letter of the law is a concern, there is no law against adding witnesses—who might include women. Because non-Jews are not bound to the religious and legal system that sanctions a Jewish marriage, some rabbis prefer and some insist that witnesses be Jewish. Even so, the addition of non-Jewish witnesses is common.

Being a guest at your wedding can be a challenge for non-Jews—especially family members who may have had little or no experience with Jewish ritual and/or feel left out or worse: some parents may need reassurance that your wedding is not a repudiation of them and everything you shared. Let them know what will happen at the ceremony and invite their questions. Send articles or videos or share this book with them; find ways to include them in the festivities in ways that are respectful of everyone's comfort level and your rabbi's parameters.

Since so many elements of a Jewish wedding are a matter of custom rather than of religion, you have many opportunities to feature and honor non-Jewish guests: they can offer the first toast, read a translation of one of the seven wedding blessings, and if your rabbi agrees, act as witnesses or sign the *ketubah*.

Showcase your family's history and traditions with

clothing, decor, and cuisine. Any kind of music can be woven into the ceremony and favorite family dishes can be served at the celebration, where virtually any cuisine can be adjusted to suit *kashrut*: Chinese, Italian, Caribbean, Southern home cooking, you name it.

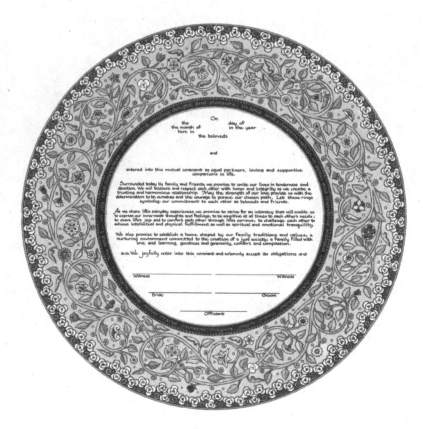

On the _____ day of _____
the month of _____ in the year _____
here in _____
the beloveds _____

and _____

entered into this mutual covenant as equal partners, loving and supportive companions in life.

Surrounded today by family and friends, we promise to unite our lives in tenderness and devotion. We will treasure and respect each other with honor and integrity as we create a trusting and harmonious relationship. May the strength of our love provide us with the determination to be ourselves and the courage to pursue our chosen path. Let these rings symbolize our commitment to each other as beloveds and friends.

As we share life's everyday experiences we promise to strive for an intimacy that will enable us to express our innermost thoughts and feelings; to be sensitive at all times to each other's needs; to share life's joy and to comfort each other through life's sorrow; to challenge each other to achieve intellectual and physical fulfillment as well as spiritual and emotional tranquility.

We also promise to establish a home shaped by our family traditions and values; a nurturing environment committed to the creation of a just society; a family filled with love, and learning, goodness and generosity, comfort and compassion.

৯৩ We joyfully enter into this covenant and solemnly accept its obligations ৯৩

Witness _____   Witness _____

Bride _____   Groom _____

Officiant _____

Joy and Happiness Ketubah
© Mickie Caspi and Caspi Art and Cards
www.caspicards.com

A Jewish Checklist

Weddings breed lists at an alarming rate, but they are essential. Entrust this inventory of ceremonial items to a reliable friend who has no other responsibilities that day: no members of the wedding party or close family.

Sample list:

- Tables and tablecloths (for *ketubah* signing and under the *huppah*)
- *Ketubah* and pen (chosen-color ink)
- *Huppah* and poles
- *Kiddush* cups and wine
- Rings
- A pouch for *Brit Ahuvim* (See page 147.)
- Candles and matches
- Wedding booklets
- *Kippot* (yarmulkes) for wedding party and guests
- Glass or glasses wrapped in napkins or pouches

Poppies Ketubah
© Jennifer Raichman
www.jenniferraichman.com

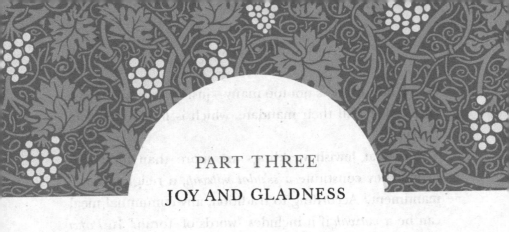

PART THREE

JOY AND GLADNESS

Celebrating Your Engagement

Reception is not the word for a Jewish celebration; even *party* misses the mark. The right word is *simcha*, which means both "joy" and a "joyous event." The purpose of Jewish wedding celebrations is to increase the joy of the couple. The Talmud says that someone who enjoys a wedding feast but does nothing to rejoice the hearts of the two beloveds has transgressed against the "five voices": the voice of joy, the voice of gladness, the voice of the bridegroom, the voice of the bride, and the voice that praises God.

From the moment two people announce their plans to marry, they take on new roles and become fiancé or fiancée, entitled to a whole season of smiles, congratulations, and *simcha.* So if one party is good, two parties are

better, and three is not too many—just as long as the celebrations fulfill their mandate, which is to gladden *your*
hearts.

Meals at Jewish weddings are more than food and
drink; they constitute a *se'udat mitzvah*, a religious commandment.[1] According to tradition, any communal meal
can be a *mitzvah* if it includes "words of Torah." In *Pirkei
Avot* (Words of the Fathers), ". . . if three have eaten at
a table and have spoken words of Torah, it is as if they
have eaten from the table of God." At the celebration of
a wedding, everything that increases a couple's happiness
fulfills a holy purpose, so "words of Torah" include remi-
niscences, toasts, and even jokes.

The decision to marry is a milestone not only for you.
Your marriage will transform your families of origin into
a newly extended family and enlarge your circle of friends.
The news of your engagement radiates outward from there;
coworkers smile and distant Facebook acquaintances send
breathless good wishes. You become stars radiating *simcha*
and setting off a season of *simchas*.

Every culture celebrates news of an impending marriage, and every generation makes those celebrations its
own. In North America, most weddings are preceded by a
round of celebrations, including engagement parties, wedding showers for both beloveds, bridal showers, bachelor
parties/weekends, bachelorette evenings/weekends, and
rehearsal dinners—all events that can range from sedate
to raucous. Although Jewish celebrations looked very different in seventeenth-century Poland and Morocco, the

common feature to this day is the giving and receiving of blessings.

TENAIM/ENGAGEMENT

The Jewish precedent/equivalent for the engagement party is a betrothal ceremony called *tenaim*, literally "conditions." From the twelfth century to the early 1800s, when families agreed on a match between their children, they signed a *tenaim* document to set the date and time of the *huppah*, to spell out financial arrangements including the dowry, and to set a penalty if either side backed out of the agreement. Finalizing the agreement was grounds for a party.

Today, the *tenaim* document and its celebration can serve as a public announcement of an engagement and the kickoff to a season of *simcha*, regardless of gender, religious status, or belief.

There has never been a *halachic* requirement for a *tenaim* document or celebration, and as family-arranged weddings became a thing of the past, they were set aside by most of the Jewish community. Where a traditional document* is in use, some couples add a clause committing the couple, the groom in particular, to seek a Jewish divorce in the event the marriage ends.

But for the most part, today's *tenaim* is less a contract

---

* See "Traditional/Orthodox Documents" in the appendix, page 181.

full of "conditions" than a witnessed statement of promises and goals for married life, such as promising to make time for each other or to attend couples counseling if the road gets rocky. Or to attend as many operas as baseball games in a given year, and to keep chocolate in the home at all times.

Your *tenaim* can be as simple as a printed sheet of paper or elaborately embellished; it can be written in any language or languages that are meaningful to you, and you can invite anyone and as many people as you like to sign as witnesses.

If you'd rather keep your promises private or if the contract format doesn't appeal, you can use the occasion to exchange sealed letters in the presence of guests—to be opened the night before the wedding or at any time you wish.

The following *tenaim* manages to be playful, reverent, and honest about the challenges and pleasures of preparing for a wedding.

CONTEMPORARY *TENAIM*

On this day, _____, which accords with the Hebrew date _____, _____ and _____ announce that they will, with God's help, stand under the huppah and make a commitment to each other on _____, which accords with the Hebrew date _____ in _____, _____.

We pledge to approach the period until that day with patience, humor, and a constant eye on the larger purpose of this event, which is to celebrate our love for each other in the presence of our community of family and friends.

We take on the task of planning this celebration with the hope that the process will deepen our relationship with each other and with our families.

If we are successful we will have united our families of origin while creating a new family of our own.

It is with gratitude and awe that we pledge ourselves to this process.

—BY RABBI LAURIE ZIMMERMAN
AND RABBI RENEE BAUER
USED WITH PERMISSION OF THE AUTHORS

Tenaim Ceremony
There are a few traditional elements, all of them yours to
use—or not—as you wish.

1. *Words of welcome, blessing, and explanation.* The traditional greeting for such an occasion is

   בָּרוּךְ הַבָּא בְּשֵׁם יְיָ.

   Baruch haba b'Shem Adonai.
   Welcome in the name of Adonai.

   Since it is likely that few, if any, of your guests
   will know what *tenaim* is all about, explain how this
   engagement party is different from most others.
   Say a few words about how a betrothal was once a
   celebration in itself, and how you have decided to
   make it your own.

2. *The announcement.* Whether or not your guests
   already know the particulars, make a "formal" pro-
   nouncement of your intention to marry:

   *We will gather at Congregation Beth El in Heartfelt
   Grove at six o'clock, the fifth of July, in the year 20**,
   which is the twelfth day in the Hebrew month of Tevet
   in the year 57**. We will meet under the huppah at
   seven p.m., where we will read our ketubah, hear the seven
   wedding blessings, exchange rings, and break a glass.*

   If all the guests at your *tenaim*/engagement
   party are invited to the wedding, you can ask them

to attend not only as guests but also as witnesses to your commitment to each other.

If any of your guests are unfamiliar with what happens at a Jewish wedding, be sure to translate and explain, which is both a good way to put them at ease and heighten their anticipation. You can also post information on your wedding website.

3. *The document.* Briefly explain that the "contract" you are about to sign has a long tradition as a legal document, which you have re-created in your own way.

   Invite someone to read the *tenaim* aloud before you both sign. Then invite your designated witnesses—as many as you wish—to add their names. If you have decided to exchange letters instead, ask everyone in the room to be a witness as you give them to each other.

4. *Light* is a universal symbol of the divine, and lighting candles is a way to invoke blessings on the couple. A room becomes warmer as well as brighter by lighting a flame and saying a few well-chosen words:

> *In the words of the Baal Shem Tov, the founder of Hasidism: "From every human being there rises a light that reaches straight to heaven. And when two souls that are destined to be together find each other, their streams of light flow together, and a single brighter light goes forth from their united being."*

Or

*As we bring together these two separate candles, we
ask that our bond be as vibrant and as illuminating as
this flame, that it continually be renewed by the strengths
of our individual selves, and that like the light from
this brighter flame, our life together may bring light and
warmth and service to our people.*

Havdalah, the brief ritual that ends Shabbat
with candles and wine, can be a setting or inspira-
tion for a *tenaim* ceremony. Just as a *havdalah* candle
represents the separation between Shabbat and the
other days of the week, lighting a candle can signify
the difference between not-married and married.
For example:
Upon lighting a candle:

*Blessed be You, Life-Spirit of the universe,
Who makes a distinction between
holy and not yet holy,
between light and darkness,
between Shabbat and the six days of the week,
between committed and uncommitted,
between common goals and personal goals,
between love and aloneness.
Blessed be you,
Who distinguishes between what is holy,
and what is not yet holy.*[2]

Blessing over fire:

בָּרוּךְ אַתָּה יְיָ, אֱלֹהֵינוּ מֶלֶךְ הָעוֹלָם, בּוֹרֵא מְאוֹרֵי
הָאֵשׁ.

Baruch atah Adonai, Eloheinu Melech Ha-olam,
borei m'orei ha'eish.
Holy One of Blessing, Your presence fills creation,
you formed the lights of fire.

Blessing over wine:

בָּרוּךְ אַתָּה יְיָ, אֱלֹהֵינוּ מֶלֶךְ הָעוֹלָם, בּוֹרֵא פְּרִי הַגָּפֶן.

Baruch atah Adonai, Eloheinu Melech Ha-olam,
borei p'ree ha'gafen.
Holy One of Blessing, Your presence fills creation
and formed the fruit of the vine.

The couple can dip their ring fingers in the wine and
place a drop on each other's lips.

5. *Building community.* To create community among
friends and family who may have never before met,
you can create a simple shared experience that will
carry over to the wedding. For example, ask guests
to bring a photograph of them with you and have
them explain where and when it was taken. Or dis-
tribute paper and pens and ask each person to
write a memory, wish, or blessing. Leave the room,
and have guests read aloud what they have written,

place the notes in a box, and seal it—to be opened
the day before or after your wedding.

Or sit in the center of a room while balls of colored yarn are distributed. Each guest ties one end
to his or her finger and the other to one or both of
you, then explains your connection and what they
treasure most about you. Eventually the room will
look like a crazy spiderweb, and people from different corners of your life will have created a web of
connection that will add even more *simcha* to your
wedding day. (Make sure you have scissors handy.)

6. *Blessings and toasts. Tenaim* is a time to receive blessings. A blessing doesn't need to be in Hebrew or to
invoke the divine. In fact, toasts are often blessings,
as in "May the two of you always be as happy as you
are tonight."

To begin (or end) a round of toasts, someone
can lead the singing of the *Shehecheyanu,* a traditional and familiar blessing of thanksgiving for all
kinds of "firsts."

בָּרוּךְ אַתָּה יְיָ, אֱלֹהֵינוּ מֶלֶךְ הָעוֹלָם, שֶׁהֶחֱיָנוּ וְקִיְּמָנוּ
וְהִגִּיעָנוּ לַזְּמַן הַזֶּה.

Baruch atah Adonai, Eloheinu Melech Ha'olam
shehecheyanu vekiamanu vehiguanu lazman hazeh.
Holy One of Blessing, Your presence fills
creation and kept us alive and preserved us
and enabled us to reach this season.

7. *The finale.* It comes with a loud crash as a plate or bowl is smashed. This old folk custom foreshadows the shattered glass that ends Jewish weddings and was probably a way to chase away evil spirits. In some communities, all the guests brought a piece of crockery to smash on the floor—outside, one supposes. More commonly, only the mothers-in-law-to-be would break a dish or plate; perhaps to celebrate that they were about to be free from the responsibility of feeding these two children.

Today, the couple tends to break a bowl bought for the occasion or a dish from each family home. You can smash anything that will break easily and make noise. Whatever you use, wrap it in a towel and slip that inside a pillowcase. You can save some of the shards to make into a memento, as some do with the shattered glass from the wedding.

Other Celebrations

If your childhood home(s) are hundreds of miles from where you're getting married, you may be feted at several gatherings given by your friends or friends of your families. These celebrations allow those who are unable to attend or won't be invited the chance to celebrate your happiness and wish you well. If it feels appropriate, you can read part of your *tenaim* or share poems or quotations at that celebration.

For the most part, American Jews have embraced the full menu of secular wedding customs. Adding a Jewish element to a shower or smoker or weekend away can be something as simple as singing *Shehecheyanu* or by creating a cookbook of favorite recipes for the Jewish holidays. Gatherings that are typically organized along gender lines can be made inclusive, especially wedding showers, which "dower" the couple with what they need. Nevertheless, men-only and women-only parties have a long history and remain popular.

For centuries and throughout the world, weddings were the only public rite of passage for women. Prewedding gatherings to celebrate, adorn, dower, and advise the bride before her wedding are probably as old as marriage itself.

Sephardic and Mizrahi Jewish communities take seriously the call to treat brides as queens, with celebrations and ceremonies beginning the week before a wedding. Female relations and friends gathered to feed the bride sweets and sing playful, romantic, and erotic songs. The bride's hands and feet are painted with henna (a natural reddish cosmetic dye that dates back to ancient Egypt) as protection against the evil eye. In some communities mothers feed their daughters seven dates or sweets to ensure strength and abundance.

Sephardic men also gather with the groom the week prior to the *huppah*, for eating, singing, and teasing. In some Ashkenazic *shtetels*, friends would carry a wedding-bound man through the streets and into the synagogue, sit him down under a canopy on the *bimah* (platform or altar), and sing to him.

The prewedding *mikveh*—immersion in a ritual bath—is a traditional requirement for brides and for the most part a private experience. However, in Sephardic communities, the bridal trip to the *mikveh* is yet another celebration, as an entourage of female relatives and friends attend the bride with songs and sweets. The custom has been adopted and adapted by Jews of all backgrounds and genders, who invite close family and friends to accompany them to the *mikveh* (or to a river or an ocean) for support and celebration. (For more about *mikveh*, see "Part Four: Getting Ready, Heart and Soul.")

THE FAMILIES

When marriages were arranged, parents knew a lot about one another before agreeing to a match. Approval of the other family was a serious consideration since a child's in-laws become your relatives, your *machetunim*. Today, parents tend to meet their prospective in-laws as a fait accompli and may have spent little or no time together before the wedding.

Whenever and however your two (or more) sets of parents meet, their anxiety will be at least as great as yours: Will they like us? Will we like them? Will we have anything in common?

Whether or not they have met before, your wedding may well be your families' first sustained interaction and can set the tone for their future relationship with each other and with you. This gives you the opportunity to lower the boundaries between "yours" and "mine" and create a new "ours."

An easy way to accomplish this is with baby pictures. Whether you're meeting at brunch or at a Friday-night Shabbat dinner or at a "rehearsal dinner" (so-called even when there is no rehearsal), by swapping photos from infancy, first birthdays, and first days at school, most parents discover they have more than enough in common; after all, they have the two of you.

A Friday-night family dinner or a Saturday-evening *havdalah* is also an opportunity for extended family to get acquainted and to recognize grandparents and other special guests by asking them to offer blessings over candles, wine, and food. Non-Jewish family members should be told about these rituals in advance and asked to participate by making a toast or adding a personal blessing.

If the family gathering is big, you might deputize a cousin or a friend to act as master of ceremonies to set a joyful tone, encourage laughter, and keep the evening moving along. (See page 96: the role of *badchan*, or wedding jester.)

Your emcee can also get people to sing. Nothing changes the temperature in a room like singing. In Eastern Europe, the prenuptial party was called *zmires*, or songs. In that setting, everyone knew the words and the melodies, but any familiar music can bring a room together: the latest pop songs, childhood and camp songs, show tunes. Just hand out the lyrics and join in.

Another way to forge family bonds is by exchanging special gifts. Traditionally these were connected to the wedding or the couple's Jewish life together: candlesticks or a *kiddush* cup they might use under the *huppah*, a *mezuzah* for the doorway of their home. The gift of a *tallis* was traditional in communities where men didn't wear a prayer shawl until marriage; today, that might take the form of a pair of matching or complementary *tallisim*.

PRAYER ON THE DAY OF BETROTHAL

> *All Merciful God!*
> *God of Love!*
> *You have created for the soul another soul*
> *To sympathize with.*
> *For the heart another heart*
> *To beat like it.*
> *Grant that I have chosen a loving, noble being.*
> *Bless my choice, O God,*
> *So that there may proceed from the union of our*
> *hearts and minds*
> *joys without number.*

—© BY DEBRA CASH
USED WITH PERMISSION

COMMUNITY

Every new household transforms the Jewish people, adding the potential for more hospitality, more generosity, and the next generation. Synagogues embrace the opportunity to rejoice with brides and grooms and bask in their reflected happiness with a communal "group hug" called an *ufruf,* which is Yiddish for "to be called up" and pronounced either *aufruf* or *oyfruf.*

In the past, a groom would be called up to the *bimah* on the Shabbat morning before his wedding and given the honor of the first *aliyah*—reciting the first blessings before the Torah reading. He would be pelted with nuts and raisins on his way back to his seat. Today, both members of the couple share this honor, and depending on their wishes and synagogue custom, they may recite the Torah blessings or read from the Torah and talk about its relevance to their union, and then take their seats under a shower of sweets.

After the service concludes, the couple, their families, friends, or congregation host a *kiddush* lunch, which might consist of coffee and bagels for everyone in attendance or a luncheon for invited guests.

In some congregations, the *ufruf* happens at Friday-evening services, where the rabbi calls the couple to the *bimah* for a blessing. The service is followed by an *Oneg Shabbat* (joy of the Sabbath), an informal gathering for schmoozing and hugging around buffet tables of food and drink.

At evening or morning services, rabbis may express the community's good wishes and recite a blessing called *Mi She'beirakh.*

MI SHE'BEIRAKH FOR BELOVEDS

May the One who blessed the marriages of our ancestors bless the forthcoming marriage of _____ and _____.

As two vines sharing a stake grow together, may your lives become joyfully intertwined.

May this union allow the Divine Spirit to shine more brightly within each of you.

May we, your friends and your community, support and nourish your relationship, fostering the growth of your love and understanding, your compassion and wisdom.

May the fruits of your labor always be sweet, and may we be able to continue to share in your joy.

Blessed are You, Adonai, Our God, Ruler of the Universe, who has kept us alive, sustained us, and enabled us to reach this season.

—BASED ON A BLESSING BY SHARON HAUSMAN COHEN
AND JANET ELIS MILDER[3]

Cottage in the Field Ketubah
© Rachel Deitsch
www.newworldketubah.com

The Wedding *Simcha*

Weddings are the biggest, most expensive and elaborate parties most people ever throw. Even relatively small and simple weddings generate what seems like countless errands and lists. Wedding websites offer planning tools to help with the details, from where to find local kosher caterers and photographers who understand the parameters of shooting in a synagogue, to descriptions of Jewish customs.

With so many e-mails, negotiations, decisions, and compromises, everyone gets overwhelmed. But if you try to remember what's important—your love for each other and a day that gladdens *your* hearts—even the most mundane preparations can take part in the sublime.

TZEDAKAH

Happy occasions are an opportunity to share your gladness with those in need. The word *tzedakah* is based on the Hebrew *tzedek*, which means "justice," and is both a holy obligation and a privilege: in other words, a *mitzvah*. Giving *tzedakah* is a way of recognizing that your greatest personal happiness is incomplete as long as the rest of the world is in need of repair.

This tradition can be honored in many ways at a wedding: you can send your floral arrangements to a hospital or nursing home after the party or donate the amount you might have spent on flowers to a cause or organization that matters to you; you can also ask that guests make a donation to a designated charity or one of their choosing, in lieu of wedding presents.

Many people share their abundance by donating 3 percent of the cost of the food to MAZON: A Jewish Response to Hunger (www.mazon.org), which funds soup kitchens, food pantries, and a wide variety of nonprofit programs in the United States and around the world.

Jewish tradition teaches that it is best to give anonymously; however, telling your guests about your generosity may encourage them to give, too, which would be another *mitzvah*. You can share your *tzedakah* plans or requests on an invitation, a wedding website, and in a wedding program.

The custom of making a donation in a multiple of eighteen ($36, $54, $1,800) is based on *gematria*, a code that assigns numerical value to Hebrew letters. The letters in the word *chai*, "life," add up to eighteen.

MENUS

Wedding food should rejoice the palates of the couple getting married. Don't order salmon if you hate it. And if carrot cake is your shared passion, get the best you can afford. Few wedding couples actually taste the food they select for their guests; there are just too many people to greet and hug to sit down for a meal. (Which is why it's a good idea to eat something during *yichud*, immediately following the ceremony. See page 159.)

There are no rules about what kind of food to serve, and there is no such thing as a single Jewish cuisine. Greek Jews put lemon in their chicken soup. Middle Eastern Jews flavor their meat with zatar and sumac. Italian Jews found a way to cure turkey so that it tasted like prosciutto. Bombay Jews favor curry. Chefs in Tel Aviv and restaurateurs in New York experiment with fresh interpretations of old standards and all-new dishes based on ethnic classics. Jewish food—like the Jewish people—is global and ever-changing. Your great-grandmother would have been horrified to see raw fish on the table.

Planning a Jewish celebration means thinking about *kashrut*—the system of laws that govern what and how Jews eat. Even if you do not keep kosher, hospitality requires taking your guests' practices into account.

Kashrut or "keeping kosher" was never considered a health measure; it was and remains a way of sanctifying the basic human need to eat. "Israel is commanded to hallow the act of eating and through this making holy, become holy."[4] The basic rules about what foods are permitted and which are forbidden are based on biblical verses, such as the rule against eating birds of prey and bottom-feeding fish. The practice of not eating meat and milk products at the same time is an elaboration on the Torah's command not to "boil a kid in its mother's milk."

In a nutshell, *kashrut* permits all vegetables and fruits,

which are categorized as *pareve*—neither milk nor meat—
and may be combined with either. Fish with fins and scales
(no shellfish) are also *pareve* and permitted. Dairy products are kosher, as are domestic fowl, and animals that
both chew their cud and have split hooves. For meat to be
kosher a blessing must be recited and the animal slaugh-
tered according to specific ritual; the meat must then
be soaked and salted to remove any trace of blood. To
observe the mandate to separate meat (*fleishig*) from dairy
(*milchig*), those foods are cooked in different pots, served
on different dishes, and are not eaten at the same meal.
The waiting period between consumption of meat and of
milk varies according to custom, from one to six hours.

Alcoholic beverages are also regulated by *kashrut*,
based on a single line in the Torah prohibiting Jews from
drinking wine that was produced for idolatrous purposes.
An ancient, complicated debate continues about what con-
stitutes kosher wine and spirits. Some synagogues require
kosher certification for wine, beer, and spirits, but many
do not. Kosher caterers will only supply products with a
hechsher, a label that indicates rabbinic supervision. Some
people like to serve Israeli wines at their *simchas*, as a way
of showing solidarity and supporting the state of Israel.

Many couples choose a vegetarian menu or serve fish
(which is *pareve*) as a way to accommodate the basics of
kashrut and make it possible to have buttercream frosting
on the cake. Vegetarian or pescaterian food satisfies many
who keep kosher; others are more comfortable with an all-
vegan or all-vegetarian menu. If your caterer is not kosher

and some of your guests require certified kosher food, you can order wrapped individual servings from a kosher market, caterer, or restaurant for them.

If you will be serving food in a synagogue, make sure you are familiar with their *kashrut* policy. Some congregations will only allow food from a list of kosher caterers; others require adherence to the basics of *kashrut*: no pork or seafood and separation of milk and meat. Many caterers are able to meet requirements for a variety of special menus.

Kosher food and catering is substantially more expensive, not only because of higher food costs but also to cover the services of a *mashgiach*, someone who supervises every aspect of its preparation and service. The term *kosher-style* usually refers to Jewish-identified foods such as matzo ball soup, but it is generally a signal that *kashrut* is not observed.

If your wedding is small, informal, or you want to minimize expenses, some caterers can be hired as "expediters" to plan a community meal. An expediter can supply recipes to family and friends, supervise their presentation, and orchestrate an elegant, delicious, and *haimish* (homey) repast.

LAUGHTER, MUSIC, AND DANCE

The goal of Jewish wedding celebrations is to rejoice the hearts of the beloveds, to make them feel as if they're on a mountaintop, as if they could fly.

The Talmud recounts the story of Samuel bar Rav Isaac, who even as a very old man would perform his wedding specialty of juggling three myrtle twigs while singing and dancing. It was said that when he died, a heavenly flame burned above his coffin as a sign of God's appreciation for his antics.[5]

That story seems to make a case not only for *simcha* but also for hilarity. It has long been customary to entertain couples with jokes, magic tricks, acrobatics, and ukulele solos: in other words, *badchanut*, "silliness," the art of the *badchan*—a joker.

For nearly seven centuries, Eastern European weddings featured this character. Sometimes called a *leytzan*, "clown," or a *marshalik*, "marshal," *badchanim* (plural) were paid professionals who sang, rhymed, posed riddles, dispensed compliments, and acted as masters of ceremonies. *Badchanim* were supposed to be learned enough to cite biblical verses and sentimental enough to elicit tears, but their primary function was to make people laugh. The *badchan* helped keep Jewish humor alive during perilous times, and the flowering of Yiddish theater and literature in the nineteenth and early-twentieth centuries is indebted to *badchanut*.

Today, the role of *badchan* can be played by friends or relatives who can tell a joke and are willing to share the spotlight. The job begins weeks if not months before the big day, recruiting guests to entertain the wedding royalty with a limerick, a puppet show, or a display of acrobatics. During the Italian Renaissance, guests composed sonnets and performed elaborate pageants and plays. At Yemenite weddings, professional singers and dancers are hired. Today, it might be a video, a PowerPoint presentation, or a poetry slam. As emcees, *badchanim* can anoint the couple as royalty with paper crowns, read messages from people who could not attend, introduce the band, and help lead blessings before and after the meal.

The *badchan* can also get people singing. Sentimental ballads, silly parodies, folk tunes, camp songs, and pop songs—any of these can turn a group of strangers into a community. Song sheets and a fearless leader can make for unforgettable serenades.

Dance is the embodiment of joy, and a beloved part of Jewish wedding celebrations. Song of Songs mentions a "dance of two companies." The Talmud asks, "How should one dance before the bride?"—and reports that Judah bar Ilai danced with a myrtle twig, while Rabbi Aha danced with the bride on his shoulders.[6]

Wedding music should get people out on the dance floor; in North America today, that's an intergenerational mix that might include Motown, disco, punk, pop, hip-hop, salsa, reggae, ballroom, and Israeli folk music, which invites dancers of all ages and abilities to join in circle dances.

The repertoire of wedding bands and DJs includes a standard Jewish medley featuring "Siman Tov U Mazel Tov," "Hava Nagila," and other klezmer songs that get just about everyone on their feet. Apart from the *hora*, a simple, easily learned circle dance, there is no special choreography, just a lot of whirling and stomping and smiling. One or two tunes are almost never enough for this kind of dance to reach its peak, so make sure your bandleader or DJ knows how to follow the mood in the room.

One of the high points—but not the end—of this portion of the *simcha* is the moment when the couple are lifted up on chairs and hold a napkin between them. The custom probably refers to the privileges of royalty, who have been carried in chairs and litters from earliest times. At Orthodox wedding parties where dancing is separated by gender, the added height allows the couple to see each other. After the couple are returned to earth, parents and grandparents are often given the same exhilarating, if somewhat terrifying, honor.

Klezmer, the music that accompanies this hilarity, has been an essential part of Ashkenazi Jewish weddings for centuries; if you wanted to disparage an event as dull, you might say it was "like a wedding without *klezmorim*" (klezmer musicians).[7] Klezmer is a mashup of folk music, popular dance tunes, military marches, and melodies by the great masters. Jewish music and dance have absorbed melodies and rhythms from around the world. Even the hora was borrowed from Romanian folk dance.

When klezmer came to America, it absorbed jazz licks and new instruments, including the clarinet. Klezmer is still alive and well and evolving, and today may be played on everything from bagpipes to electric guitars, powered by rock rhythms.

The music and its communal invitation to dance

requires no introduction, but klezmer includes a lot of up-tempo dance tunes called *freylachs*, "happies," with specialty numbers especially for weddings, such as the *Bobbes Tanz* for grandmothers. If you like, an emcee, DJ, or *badchan* can announce and explain:

The Mitzvah Tanz, dancing with the bride is considered a *mitzvah*, so everyone tries to take a turn with her, beginning with her father.

The Machetunim Tanz, for parents of the couple.

The Huppah Tanz, in which friends hold a *tallis* or a tablecloth above the couple and dance around them.

The Besem *(broom)* Tanz, where a broom is used as a prop—ridden as a horse, played as a guitar, or balanced on a dancer's forehead or chin.

The Flash *(bottle)* Tanz, which involves dancing with a bottle on the head.

The Kazatsky, a Cossack dance with deep-knee-bend kicks, which turns into a contest of strength and endurance.

The Mezinke, a tribute to parents (traditionally mothers) who have just brought the last of their children to the *huppah*. Parents sit on a chair while the company dances around them.

The Krenzl *(crown),* guests dance around the parents (traditionally mothers), who are crowned with a wreath of flowers.

PHOTOGRAPHY/VIDEOGRAPHY

No religious rule forbids photography or videography under the *huppah,* but this is something to clear with your rabbi. Some clergy feel it is intrusive and distracts from the sanctity of the moment, and some synagogues have policies that prohibit picture taking. A good photographer/ videographer can minimize disruption and ensure you get the pictures you want. The best of them become valued and helpful members of the wedding party.

Websites and portfolios are a good place to begin your search for photographers and videographers, but skill is only one factor. It's helpful if they have experience with Jewish weddings and are familiar with the vocabulary (*huppah, klezmer*) and customs, such as signing the *ketubah.* Some photographers (Jewish and not Jewish) make a specialty of Jewish weddings. Some Jewish-owned studios cater to Orthodox families who prefer to have both a male and a female photographer for pictures at women-only and men-only gatherings.

Face-to-face interviews with wedding photographers are essential; they should insist on meeting you before agreeing to work for you. Because they will have access to private, behind-the-scenes moments, you need people with whom you can collaborate and communicate. People you like.

Good chemistry is important, but pay attention to promptness, courtesy, and flexibility as well. Check references. Even if your best friends rave about someone, contact a few couples you don't know.

Circle of Life Ketubah
© Celia Lemonik
Image courtesy of www.ketubah.com

PART FOUR

GETTING READY, HEART AND SOUL

A wedding is a milestone and a turning point that resets your life's trajectory. It is also an encounter with whatever you consider sacred.

The crush of decisions and details usually overwhelms the spiritual dimensions of a wedding, but some rituals and customs allow you to slow down and consider the meaning of this new beginning.

Mikveh

Without water there is no life. Water rituals symbolize purification and transformation and are part of virtually every spiritual tradition on the planet. According to the Talmud, the source of all water is the river that originated in Eden, the place where life began, and thus that element can make us feel whole and renewed. *Mikveh* is the preeminent water ritual for Jews. Done with intention and accompanied by

prayers, immersion in a *mikveh* enacts a change of status—
such as the change from not-married to married.

Mikveh, literally "a gathering" or "a collection of water,"
can refer to any body of running water; spring-fed ponds
and lakes, rivers, and the oceans are natural *mikva'ot*.
Mikveh is also the name for an indoor pool specially con-
structed for the purpose of ritual immersion, and the
name of a building that houses the pool.

The ritual is simple; after bathing, you descend, nude,
into the water and immerse completely, every inch of skin
and strand of hair submerged. You say a blessing, immerse
two more times, and walk up the seven steps and begin anew.

For centuries, Jewish brides have immersed to prepare
for their wedding nights, traditionally the beginning of
sexual intimacy and also the start of monthly immersions
following menstruation.[*] Today, the prewedding *mikveh*
has been embraced by the larger Jewish community that
has recognized and reclaimed the beauty of the ritual and
power at a time of transformation.

No two *mikva'ot* look the same. Some are located in
freestanding facilities, others in synagogues, schools, or
renovated houses. The decor ranges from utilitarian to
elegant. Some are for women only, some for men only, and
some welcome the full diversity of the Jewish community.
Your rabbi can describe your local options.

---

[*]This monthly practice called *niddah* or *taharah mishpachah*, once the
purview of married Orthodox women, has been adopted by Jews of
all descriptions, including some same-sex couples and some husbands
before reuniting with their wives.

Call ahead and make an appointment for your immersion and ask about the expected fee or donation. Most *mikva'ot* provide toiletries, towels, and hair dryers, but check to make sure if you should bring anything. Ask if you can bring friends or family, and, if you wish, whether one of them can act as your witness. If you've never seen the *mikveh*, ask if you can arrange a tour a few weeks in advance.

Most *mikva'ot* employ a person or people who care for the facility and act as witnesses. The role of the witness is to help ensure that your immersion is kosher, which only means making sure there are no impediments to the water's touching every inch of your skin and watching to see that your entire body is submerged. Because *mikveh* is not considered a *mitzvah* for men, they require no witness, and in all likelihood none will be offered, but you can ask a friend or family member to act as your witness.

Mikveh immersions and blessings take only a few minutes. Careful preparation is what makes the experience meaningful; before you go, turn off your electronics, gather your thoughts, take a walk, meditate, or write in a journal if you keep one. Bring a favorite poem or reading with you.

Expect to be at the *mikveh* for about an hour. Most of that time will be spent in the bathroom, where you will find a checklist of what and how to scrub, floss, trim, shampoo, and brush. This is not about cleanliness but to make sure no barriers exist between you and the water. These ablutions can become a spiritual preparation for immersion and marriage if you treat them as a *kavanah*— an intention or way to remain mindful of the moment.

SEVEN KAVANOT—BODY, MIND, AND SPIRIT

HINENI. Here I am. *Take a minute and think about the transition* mikveh *will help you mark today.* Immersion in the *mikveh* represents a spiritual transformation from one state to another. Breathe deeply. Sigh audibly.

HIDDUR MITZVAH. The unadorned body is beautiful in itself. *Remove all jewelry as well as makeup, paying special attention to the eyes. Remove nail polish on fingers and toes. (Acrylics may remain if they have been on for more than a month.)* There is no need for adornment or artifice in the *mikveh.* There should be no physical barriers between the body and the living waters.

NEKAVIM NEKAVIM. You fashioned the human being intricate in design. *Empty your bladder.* Jewish tradition celebrates and blesses the body in every possible moment and mode.

B'TZELEM ELOHIM. I am made in the image of God. *Remove all clothing, eyeglasses, contact lenses, dental plates, hearing aids.* People enter the *mikveh* as naked as the day they were born, without rank or status. Each of us simply a human being. Each of us gloriously a human being.

ELOHAI NESHAMA SHENATATA BI TEHORAH HI. The soul in me is pure. *Shower or bathe with thoughtful attention to the miracle of your body. Pay attention to every part of yourself.*

Wash yourself, head to toe: shampoo your hair; lather your shoulders, back, arms, belly, and genitals. Scrub elbows, knees, and heels, removing calluses and dead skin. Wash between fingers and toes. Relax and enjoy. The water of the *mikveh* will feel even sweeter after this.

KOL HANESHAMA T'HALEL YAH. The breath of every living thing praises You. *Clean your ears, blow your nose, brush and floss your teeth, rinse your mouth.* Stand before the mirror. Consider all of your senses. Look into your eyes and smile. Think about the words that come from your mouth.

TIKKUN OLAM. We can stand for justice. We can build a world of peace and justice. *Clean under your nails—toenails, too. (Nails do not need to be cut.)* Consider the power of your hands and feet to create wholeness in your life, in our world.

When you enter the mikveh *do not rush. Walk slowly. Count the seven steps into the water, stopping on each one. Relax into the embrace of the water, into whatever the next moment may hold for you.*

—CREATED BY AND REPRODUCED WITH THE
BLESSING OF MAYYIM HAYYIM LIVING WATERS,
MAYYIMHAYYIM.ORG

Once you enter the water, take a breath, release it, and submerge completely. Open your hands. Listen to the beating of your heart. You need only stay under for a moment or two. After rising from the water, your witness pronounces the immersion *kasher* (complete). Recite the blessing for immersion and then immerse two more times. It is customary to follow the second or third immersion with a *Shehecheyanu*, the blessing of thanksgiving, but there are no mandated prayers; you can make up your own or just enjoy the quiet. (See page 111 for a prewedding *mikveh* ceremony.)

Some people prefer to go to the *mikveh* alone or accompanied only by a parent, close friend, or their beloved, creating a quiet island in time to reflect and relax. Others bring an entourage to greet them after immersing with song and to celebrate, following the custom of Sephardic communities, where female family members and friends sing to the bride on her way to the *mikveh* and follow the immersion with more music, food (especially sweets), and the application of henna.

Whatever your choice, don't underestimate the power of this ritual. Plan the day so you don't go back to work. Let the experience soak in.

Creating a meaningful immersion is possible even if the closest community *mikveh* is hundreds of miles away, or if the *mikveh* near you is not accessible or welcoming. (Unfortunately some traditional *mikva'ot* still turn away LGBTQ Jews and challenge the religious status of others; people who are not Jewish are not permitted to immerse except for the purpose of conversion to Judaism.)

You can immerse outdoors in the ocean, a river, or a stream-fed lake or pond—climate and weather permitting. The beauty of the natural world and the experience of fresh water add a memorable dimension to the experience. Modesty and privacy can be maintained by choosing a secluded spot and immersing early in the morning or after dark. You can enter the water in a bathing suit and slip out of it before the immersions and blessings, while surrounded by friends who can testify that your immersion was complete and proper.

When weather or climate make an outdoor *mikveh* impossible, people have improvised and immersed in swimming pools, hot springs, and hot tubs. These are not kosher immersion pools, but with thoughtful preparation, *kavanah*, and the support of loving friends and family, the spiritual and emotional power of *mikveh* is present.

Another water ceremony, modeled on the Jewish tradition of washing hands before meals, is available to everyone. Pouring water over the hands has nothing to do with hygiene. It echoes the practice of priests in ancient Israel, who washed as a form of spiritual preparation before entering the Temple.

The following ceremony can be done day or night, indoors or outside, by anyone—Jewish or not. You can pour the water yourself or have someone do it for you; consider using "natural" water from a spring, river, or sea. Take time to find a beautiful pitcher or a laver, the two-handled cup used for washing, and have a new white towel ready.

HAND-WASHING CEREMONY
BEFORE A WEDDING

Water sustains the ongoing miracle of creation.
From the invisible transport of blood and lymph
to the mighty energies of tides,
to the clouds that feed the planet.
All of it sacred: the kiss, the tear, the flow,
my own liquid body: sacred.

Remove watches, bracelets, rings, and nail polish. Wash your hands carefully, clean beneath your nails.

Pour water over your open palms. *I open my hands to receive the blessings of marriage.*

Pour water over your closed hands. *I close my hands and think of what matters most: my beloved's hand in mine.*

Pour water over the backs of your hands. *I cannot hold running water any more than I can stop time, but this moment is mine forever.*

Pour water into your cupped hands. *I am filled to overflowing by the miracle of my life and the joy of my love.*

With clean hands and a pure heart, I am ready to become one with another, to share the joys of life with my beloved, to teach and to learn the lessons of married life.

MIKVEH CEREMONY BEFORE MARRIAGE

BEFORE IMMERSION

Kavanot for preparation:

> *Immersion in water softens our form,*
> *Making us malleable,*
> *Dissolving some of the rigidity of who we are.*
> *This allows us to decide who we wish to be when we*
> *come out of the water.*
> *The water changes us neither by washing away*
> *something*
> *Nor by letting something soak into us,*
> *But simply by softening us*
> *So that we can choose*
> *To remold ourselves into a different image.**

or

> *Water is God's gift to living souls, to cleanse us, to*
> *purify us, to sustain and renew us through the*
> *stages of our life's journey.*
> *I am now prepared*
> *To leave behind that which I no longer choose*
> *To become one with another life,*
> *To become a creator of new possibilities*
> *To become a partner in sharing the joys of life,*
> *To teach and to learn the lessons of married life.†*

---

* The National Center for Learning and Leadership, CLAL.
† Rabbi Barbara Penzner and Amy Small.

Immediately prior to entering the water:

> As I immerse, I begin a new stage in my life. May my
> entry into the waters of the mikveh strengthen me for
> the journey that lies ahead.*

or

> Now, as I immerse myself, I begin a new stage, a phase
> of rebirth and renewal of Your world and Your
> people Israel. I prepare for my new life and for the
> sanctification of that life through kiddushin, Your
> holy state of marriage.

יִהְיוּ לְרָצוֹן אִמְרֵי־פִי, וְהֶגְיוֹן לִבִּי לְפָנֶיךָ,
יְהֹוָה, צוּרִי וְגֹאֲלִי.

Y'hiyu l'ratzon imray-fee v'heg-yon leebee
l'fanecha: Adonai, tzuree v'go-alee.
May the words of my mouth and the
meditations of my heart be acceptable to You,
Adonai, my Rock and my Redeemer.

FIRST IMMERSION

*Submerge your body so that every part of you is covered. After you
emerge, recite the blessing for immersion:*

---

*From a ceremony created by Matia Rania Angelou, Deborah Issokson, and Judith D. Kummer for Mayyim Hayyim Living Waters.

בָּרוּךְ אַתָּה יְיָ, אֱלֹהֵינוּ מֶלֶךְ הָעוֹלָם, אֲשֶׁר קִדְּשָׁנוּ
בְּמִצְוֹתָיו, וְצִוָּנוּ עַל הַטְּבִילָה.

Baruch atah Adonai, Eloheinu Melech Ha-olam,
asher kid-shanu b'mitzvo-tav, v'tzi-vanu al ha-tevilah.
Praised are You, Adonai, God of all Creation,
who sanctifies us with Your commandments and
commanded us concerning immersion.

SECOND IMMERSION

Immerse again and after you rise from the water recite:

> *I will betroth you to me forever. I will betroth you to me*
> *with righteousness and with justice, with goodness*
> *and with compassion. I will betroth you to me in*
> *truth; and we will come to know God.**

AFTER THIRD IMMERSION

> *My God, Creator and Sustainer of all life, may I step*
> *forth into a life filled with continued wisdom and*
> *deeds of kindness.*
> *May I step forward into a life filled with the blessings of*
> *new beginnings.*
> *May I be a loving mate, partner, and friend to my*
> *beloved.*
> *Be with me as I enter this new time in my life.*

---

* Hosea 2:19–20.

*May You, God, Who has blessed my coming forth into
this day, bless my going out into life, fulfillment,
and peace.**

or

*May the words of my mouth, the meditations of my heart,
and this act of sanctification seal my devotion to a
life of Torah, Avodah, and Gemilut Hasadim; a life
of learning Your ways, a life of standing in Your
presence, a life made holy by acts of loving-kindness.*†

—CREATED BY AND REPRODUCED WITH
THE BLESSING OF MAYYIM HAYYIM LIVING
WATERS, MAYYIMHAYYIM.ORG

---

* Charlotte Goldberg *Mikveh*, Cleveland.
† Congregation Beth El of the Sudbury River Valley.

The Blessing of Memory

The joy of a wedding can summon memories and complicated feelings as you think of people who would have been at your wedding "if only they had lived long enough." Sadness, anger, or guilt may surface and cast a shadow over your happiness. The custom of visiting the graves of loved ones before a wedding can be a cathartic way to acknowledge loss, to share memories with your intended, and to let go of regrets and past grievances.

There is no need to say or do anything at the cemetery. Jews leave pebbles as a token of remembrance because rather than flowers that wither, the stones remain. You can, however, bring a poem or write a remembrance to read aloud. If your beloved accompanies you, bring a photograph that captures a memory to share. If the cemetery is too far away to visit, set aside time for reminiscing, leaf through a family photo album, listen to music the deceased loved.

You are remembered in love.
You are part of the now in me.
All the good
All the love
All the comfort a person can give
Is remembered

And repeated
For your sake.
Time changes
Everything passes
But love.
Peace abide you.[1]

—GERRY DICKER

Other losses may surface, too. For people who have experienced the death of a partner, divorce, or the end of a long-term relationship, immersion can be a way of making a final separation with the past, as can the Rosh Hashanah/New Year custom of *taschlich*. Casting bread into a body of moving water is a way to symbolically let go of the past and make a fresh start.

Fasting and Prayer

It is customary for the wedding couple to separate from each other for a time before the wedding. This has nothing to do with superstitions about bad luck, since grooms traditionally saw their brides before the *huppah* at a veiling ceremony or a *ketubah* signing.

A brief separation—a week, a day, or just the night before the wedding—carves out time for rest and recovery; it's also a way to step back from the inevitable tensions that arise between you. Take the time to be alone or spend it with a few of your nearest and dearest. Even a brief separation heightens anticipation for the day and night ahead.

Judaism is not big on self-denial, and fast days are few[*] and prohibited if health is a concern. For Jews, fasting is not about the mortification of the flesh but is a way to heighten appreciation of and gratitude for food and drink.

Couples sometimes fast on their wedding day—though a half-day fast is advisable if the wedding starts late in the evening. As on Yom Kippur, abstaining from food symbol-

---

[*] Fasting is not allowed on holidays and semiholidays including Shavuot, Sukkot, Hanukkah, and Purim; the fifteenth day of Av and the fifteenth day of Shevat; Rosh Hodesh, the first day of the Jewish month, except Rosh Hodesh Nissan; and Isru Chag, the day after the final days of Passover.

izes a new start. It is said that a couple fasts in preparation for their covenant with each other just as the people of Israel fasted on the day that the Torah was given to them.

The couple breaks their fast with the first cup of wine under the *huppah*. After the ceremony they take their first meal together—serving each other—as a married couple.

Weddings summon a lot of spontaneous prayer: pleas for good weather, supplication that the caterer will get everything right, gratitude for having found the love of one's life.

There are two formal prayers that seem appropriate for a wedding couple, one about starting over, another about starting out. The *Viddui* is a public prayer of confession recited on Yom Kippur by the whole community and also at the end of life. This version seeks forgiveness for interpersonal failings:

> *I have been quick to anger with my family and*
> *I have been afraid to show them my love.*
> *I have failed to listen to my teachers.*
> *I have spoken too loudly to my beloved.*
> *I have hurt others.*
> *I have allowed others to be hurt without reaching out to*
>   *help.*
> *I have lied to myself and to others.*
> *I have forgotten my better self.*
> *I turn to those I have hurt and ask their forgiveness.*

I turn to those who have hurt me and forgive them.
I turn within and forgive myself.[2]

The prayer for travelers, *T'filat HaDerech*, seeks blessings on the start of a shared journey:

> *May it be Your will*
> *Adonai our God and God of our ancestors,*
> *to lead us in safety, to direct our steps in safety,*
> *to guide us in safety,*
> *and enable us to reach our destination*
> *in life, in joy, and in peace, and bring us back home in*
> *   peace.*[3]

Persian Silk Ketubah
© Mickie Caspi and Caspi Cards & Art
www.caspicards.com

Before the *Huppah*

Over the centuries, Jews have surrounded weddings with parties and rituals galore. The run-up to the big day sees *tenaim*, *zmires*, and *mikveh*—a crescendo of *simcha*, anticipation, and *kavanah* (spiritual intention) that continues right up to the moment a couple steps under the wedding canopy.

The pre-*huppah* customs of *tish*, *bedeken*, and *ketubah* are sometimes referred to, collectively, as *kabbalat panim*, "welcoming the faces." None of these traditions are required; they are not *mitzvot* (commandments) but customs, yours to choose or change or dispense with.

A traditional *kabbalat panim* begins with separate festivities for bride and groom. The *chossen's tish* (groom's table) is for male guests—either a small circle of family and friends or all the men invited to the wedding. The groom is expected to offer comments about the Torah portion of the week, but this is usually a pretext for friends to interrupt, sing, and tease him. Refreshments, including alcohol, are served.

Meanwhile, the bride is in another room for *hachnasat kallah* (welcoming the bride) with female relatives, friends, and guests. She is seated on a platform or decorated chair as befits her status as wedding royalty, and her guests might sing and dance for her, give blessings and sometimes flowers. Refreshments are served.

Eventually, the bride sends a delegation to invite the men for the *bedeken* (veiling). The groom is usually carried in on a chair, accompanied by singing friends and family. This may be the first time the couple have seen each other for a day or more.

The custom of having the groom lower the veil over the bride's face has been understood as a way for the groom to ensure that he is marrying the one he loves, avoiding the mistake made by Jacob, who married the veiled Leah instead of Rachel, his intended.[1] However, in an earlier passage, Rebecca takes the initiative and covers herself with a veil in preparation for meeting Isaac, who will become her husband.[2] In fact, this story is the source of the traditional greeting to the bride at a *bedeken*:

$$\text{אֲחֹתֵינוּ אַתְּ הֲיִי לְאַלְפֵי רְבָבָה.}$$

Achoteinu: aht hayee l'alfay rehvavah.
Our sister: may you be the mother
of thousands of myriads.

This is followed by the threefold (priestly) benediction:

May God make you like Sarah, Rebecca, Rachel, and
Leah. May God bless you and keep you. May God make
the Countenance shine upon you and be gracious to you.
May God lift the Countenance upon you and give you
peace.

If the *ketubah* has yet to be signed, it is read aloud and
signed by two witnesses. Musicians start to play, which
begins the procession to the *huppah*.

Today, these customs have been adopted, revised, and
personalized to reflect the lives and values of marrying
couples. A contemporary *kabbalat panim* might look like
this:

The beloveds, who have been separated for a day and
a night, are accompanied by their attendants into a room
full of family and friends, who greet them by singing a
wordless melody (*niggun*) taught to them by the rabbi or
cantor. According to a Hasidic saying, "When two who
cannot sing raise their voices together, a miracle happens."

The couple are seated facing each other at a table, a
tish. The rabbi welcomes everyone, explains the meaning
of the *ketubah*, and reads it aloud in Hebrew. A friend reads
the English translation, and the couple, rabbi, and at least
two witnesses then sign the document.

The rabbi gives the beloveds letters they were asked
to write to each other months before the wedding. They
unseal and read them aloud to each other.

For the *bedeken*, the couple wrap one another in prayer

shawls while the guests sing the *niggun* that greeted them earlier.

A violinist starts to play and the processional begins.

PROCESSIONAL

Accompanying a couple to the *huppah* is a joyful *mitzvah* and even a communal responsibility. Rabbi Judah bar Il'ai instructed his students to put aside their studies to accompany a poor bride to her canopy.[3] In European *shtetels* and Israeli *kibbutzim*, nearly everyone who could walk would join the procession.

Jewish wedding attendants are called *shushvinim* or "friends," a term applied to Gabriel and Michael, the angels who attended the wedding of Adam and Eve. Traditionally, each member of the couple has two *shushvinim*—the Yiddish term is *unterfuhrers*, "accompaniers"—who not only march in the processional but also take care of tasks such as holding the *ketubah* during the ceremony and escorting the couple on their way from the *huppah* to *yichud*.

Jewish wedding processionals differ from secular and Christian weddings in that typically both (all) parents escort their children to the *huppah*. However, there is no required order, but in general:

🌱 If the *huppah* is to be handheld, it begins the procession, carried by those who will hold it during the ceremony.

🐝 Rabbi and/or cantor.

🐝 Attendants, in pairs, singly, and/or as escorts for grandparents, siblings, and other honored guests.

🐝 Finally, the couple are escorted to the *huppah* by their parents, who leave them with a kiss.

The complexity of modern families sometimes requires alternative choreography. Divorced/remarried parents and children from previous marriages often take part in the processional; if they are on good terms and everyone is willing, birth/adoptive parents can still accompany their child, who remains proof of a dream they once shared. Children of previous marriages can be escorted by attendants or, depending on age and willingness, can accompany their parents.

If there are too many competing claims, the couple can avoid conflict by entering side by side. This also does away with giving the "grand finale" to the last person (and, traditionally, her dress) down the aisle, which is an anachronism for egalitarian and same-sex couples.

Music makes all the difference. Even before the processional, soft prelude or welcoming music creates a sense of calm anticipation that helps guests settle and quiet down. Processional music is stately but not somber. Cantors sometimes sing musical settings of poems from the Song of Songs, including "*Dodi Li*" (I Am My Beloved's), "*Iti*

Mil'Vanon" (Come with Me from Lebanon), and *"Hanava Babanot"* (Beautiful One). Instrumental music can be selected from a vast and varied catalog that includes classical pieces, Yiddish folk songs, Ladino songs, Israeli folk or pop songs, and contemporary music. If one or both members of the couple are heir to another musical tradition, a Gallic melody or the sound of a Chinese pipa is a beautiful and thoughtful touch.

Cantors are the best resource for Jewish music and can act as musical coordinators for the whole wedding day, including the *simcha.* They can also recommend local musicians for the ceremony, as well as bands and even DJs for the party.

During the processional at evening weddings, attendants sometimes carry candles lighting the way to the *huppah.* Guests can create a widening circle of light with flameless candles, set out on chairs.

Some rabbis ask that the couple provide a pair of candlesticks for the table under or near the *huppah.* No blessing is said for candles at a wedding, but if you wish to light them, a family member or friend can read this passage, attributed to the Baal Shem Tov:

> From every human being there rises a light that reaches straight to heaven. And when two souls that are destined for each other find one another, their streams of light flow together and a single brighter light goes forth from their united being.[4]

CIRCLING

The custom of the bride's circling the groom before they entered the *huppah* is attributed to the phrase from the book of Jeremiah. "A woman shall go around a man."[5] With this act, the bride created a symbolic wall to protect the groom from evil spirits, from the glances of other women, and from the temptations of the world. It also signaled that the couple's primary allegiance was shifting from their parents to each other.[6] For the mystics, circling was a way for a bride to enter the groom's *sefirot*—spheres of the human soul that correspond to the seven lower attributes of God.

The bride—sometimes led by both mothers—made either three or seven circuits around the groom. The preference for three was based on the threefold biblical phrase "I will betroth you to me forever. I will betroth you to me in righteousness, and in justice, and in loving-kindness, and in compassion; and I will betroth you to me in faithfulness."[7] Also, husbands were required to fulfill three obligations to their wives: to provide food and clothing and conjugal relations.

The number seven has special resonance at a wedding: the world was created in seven days; seven wedding blessings are recited under the *huppah*; and marriage is a seven-days-a-week act of creation.

Circling, which had long been discarded because of its suggestion of the bride's subservience, has come back into use—not only reclaimed but redefined. It can symbolize the space a couple will share, mutual circling (making circuits around each other, or holding hands and walking in a circle) celebrates the creation of a new household where each partner protects and supports the other. Some couples add a reading to the ritual:

HAKAFOT: CIRCLING

May we be loving and generous with one another.
May we find strength to face life's challenges.
May we seek balance in our lives and harmony in our home.
May we always nurture each other's passions.
May we see beauty in all places and in all people.
May our lives be founded on truth and commitment to justice.
May we be fully present to each other and to the wonder of life.[8]

Under the *Huppah*

Before the eleventh century, a Jewish marriage required two ceremonies: the first was betrothal, called *erusin* or *kiddushin*, from the same root as *kadosh*, "holy," and included a formal contract. After this, the bride and the groom were considered legally bound to each other, and even though no physical intimacy was allowed, a bill of divorce was necessary to end the relationship.

The second ceremony, which finalized the marriage, was called *nissuin*, from the verb "to carry," as the bride was "carried" to her new home and sexual intimacy was permitted.

The separation of *kiddushin* and *nissuin/huppah* ended during the eleventh century for practical reasons: two separate ceremonies meant two separate banquets, which was a financial hardship for all but the wealthiest. Also, those were perilous times for Jews, so if a betrothed groom died or was deported during the intervening months, his bride became *agunah*, a woman who was unable to marry. Finally, since many grooms lived with the bride's family before the *huppah*, a single ceremony removed the temptations faced by betrothed couples, who were forbidden to touch.

Contemporary Jewish weddings retain traces of both

ceremonies, but the passage of time has smoothed away the edges so that today it feels like a seamless arc from betrothal and rings to seven blessings and broken glass.

BLESSINGS AND RINGS

Welcome
The wedding begins with two greetings, usually chanted or sung by the rabbi or cantor. The words come from Psalms and the first one is addressed to the beloveds under the *huppah* and to everyone in attendance:

בָּרוּךְ הַבָּא בְּשֵׁם יְיָ.

Baruch haba b'Shem Adonai.
Welcome in the name of Adonai.

The second welcome blessing invokes God's presence:

בֵּרַכְנוּכֶם מִבֵּית יְיָ.

Bayrachnuchem mi'beyt Adonai.
Welcome in this house of Adonai.

After the welcome, the rabbi or cantor recites or chants still more words of blessing, called *Mi Adir*:

מִי אַדִּיר עַל הַכֹּל,

מִי בָּרוּךְ עַל הַכֹּל,

מִי גָּדוֹל עַל הַכֹּל,

יְבָרֵךְ אֶת־הֶחָתָן וְאֶת־הַכַּלָּה.

Mi adir al hakol,
Mi baruch al hakol,
Mi gadol al hakol,
Y'vareich et hachatan v'ethakallah.
Splendor is upon everything
Blessing is upon everything
Who is full of this abundance
Bless these loving companions.[9]

As part of the welcome, some rabbis instruct the guests about their role as witnesses, to rejoice and honor the couple on their wedding day and also to be a sustaining community for them. Since weddings are thought to increase the potential for peace and holiness in the world, rabbis may also offer a prayer that this marriage will be a source of blessing in the world.

Blessing (Kiddush) for the First Cup of Wine*

There is a saying, "Without wine there is no blessing." *Kiddush* is how Jews sanctify virtually all Jewish holidays and

---

*Wine can be replaced with grape juice, which is also "fruit of the vine."

personal observances, and in a wedding it is repeated twice. It is customary for the rabbi or cantor to chant *kiddush*, and for the couple to respond, "Amen." However, the wine is not drunk until after the blessing of betrothal later in the ceremony.

בָּרוּךְ אַתָּה יְיָ, אֱלֹהֵינוּ מֶלֶךְ הָעוֹלָם, בּוֹרֵא פְּרִי הַגָּפֶן.

Baruch atah Adonai, Eloheinu Melech Ha-olam,
borei p'ree ha'gafen.
Holy One of the Blessing, Your presence fills creation,
forming the fruit of the vine.

It is traditional to use two cups, one for each time that *kiddush* is recited under the *huppah*, and some couples borrow a glass or goblet from each family. Reviving an old European custom, Jewish artisans create special cups or matched pairs for weddings, which can become treasured ritual objects at home.

Betrothal Blessings / Birkat Erusin

Because this blessing was once recited a full year before the *huppah*, it included a specific warning that the couple were not permitted sexual relations until after the *huppah* ceremony (*kiddushin*). The blessing is chanted or read in Hebrew by the rabbi or cantor. Because its content is no longer relevant and is addressed solely to the groom, it is often given a freer translation.[10]

בָּרוּךְ אַתָּה יְיָ, אֱלֹהֵינוּ מֶלֶךְ הָעוֹלָם, אֲשֶׁר קִדְּשָׁנוּ
בְּמִצְוֹתָיו, וְצִוָּנוּ עַל הָעֲרָיוֹת, וְאָסַר לָנוּ אֶת הָאֲרוּסוֹת,
וְהִתִּיר לָנוּ אֶת הַנְּשׂוּאוֹת לָנוּ עַל יְדֵי חֻפָּה וְקִדּוּשִׁין.

Blessed are You, the Eternal our God, the sovereign of all worlds,
who has made us holy through mitzvot *and has instructed us*
to honor the sacredness of sexual intimacy and has restrained
us from being intimate with those who are committed to others,
but has permitted us to wed under the huppah *and in holiness.*
Blessed are You, the Eternal, who makes the people Israel holy
through the huppah *and the sacredness of marriage.*[11]

or

Blessed are You, our God, Source of Life, who frees us from fear
and shame and opens us to the holiness of our bodies and their
pleasures. You guide us to entwine our hearts in righteousness,
justice, loving-kindness, and compassion. Blessed are You, who
sanctifies Israel through love that is honorable and true.[12]

After this blessing, the couple drink from one of the goblets and the cup may be offered to parents and grandparents, who might be remembering another *kiddush*, at a son's *bris* (ritual circumcision) or a daughter's naming or *brit* (covenant) ceremony, events where parents pray that their children will grow into a life of study (Torah), a loving relationship (*huppah*), and good works (*gemilut hasadim*). Sharing the wine in this way is often done without explanation, but sometimes the rabbi will acknowledge it.

> We are grateful to you, Source of all Creation, for the loving care and teaching of parents, the ties of heart and mind and memory that link brothers and sisters, and for the friendships that fill our cup to overflowing.[13]

The Ring Ceremony

The legal enactment of a Jewish wedding (*kinyan*) is the giving and accepting of a ring with a nine-word phrase of consecration:

הֲרֵי אַתְּ מְקֻדֶּשֶׁת לִי בְּטַבַּעַת זוּ כְּדַת מֹשֶׁה וְיִשְׂרָאֵל.

Haray aht m'kudeshet li b'taba'at tzu k'dat Moshe v'Yisrael.
By this ring you are holy to me (as my wife) in accordance with the traditions of Moses and Israel.

This formula, *haray aht*, contains thirty-two letters that, according to *gematria*, spell the word *heart—lev*. Because it is considered essential that both members of the couple understand its meaning, *haray aht* is always recited both in Hebrew and the vernacular language of the community.

Traditionally, only the groom recites this phrase. The bride is not required to say or do anything when she accepts the ring, although the absence of a liturgical response has been interpreted as permission for her to add a response. Some use a biblical phrase: "I will betroth you to me forever, in righteousness, in justice, in love, mercy, and faith-fulness" or "I am my beloved's and my beloved is mine." Some make a statement of assent: "In accepting this ring, I am holy to you as your wife in accordance with the tradi-tions of Moses and Israel."

For most Jews today, however, the ring ceremony has become an equal exchange of rings and of the *haray aht*, pronouns corrected for gender, sometimes adding the name of Miriam, the prophet: ". . . in accordance with the traditions of Moses and Miriam (*umiryam*)."

הֲרֵי אַתָּה מְקֻדָּשׁ לִי בְּטַבַּעַת זוּ כְּדָת מֹשֶׁה וְיִשְׂרָאֵל.

Haray atah m'kudash li b'taba'at tzu k'dat Moshe v'Yisrael.
By this ring you are consecrated to me (as my
husband) in accordance with the traditions
of Moses (*uMiryam*) and Israel.

It was customary to place the ring on the right index finger, a practice that may stem from an ancient belief that the index finger was connected directly to the heart. Put-ting the ring on the index finger also made it easier for wit-nesses to see that the bride had accepted the ring freely and as a public transaction—not as a gift.

Today, many couples forgo this custom and put the

---

*For Orthodox Jews, an exchange is not the same *kinyan*, and these actions could jeopardize the *halachic* validity of the marriage. The bride can give the groom a ring as a gift, but only when and where it could not be construed as *kinyan*.

ring directly on the finger where it will be worn, as a symbol of love and commitment. Others find it more meaningful to move the ring from the index to the ring finger, which adds agency to acceptance.

The ring ceremony completes the betrothal/*kiddushin* part of the wedding.

Ketubah Reading

The *ketubah* is usually read next, before the second glass of wine is blessed. (In all other rituals, *kiddush* is recited only once; the inclusion of this second blessing is the "seam" where two separate ceremonies were joined together.)

The rabbi usually reads the *ketubah* in Hebrew and/or English. If the *ketubah* is written as a series of promises, the couple might read it to each other.

After the *ketubah* reading, some couples invite family members and close friends to read a poem or prayer or have all the guests read aloud from a wedding booklet. If this is your choice, make sure to keep it brief. The liturgy is not long, and too many additions can overwhelm and slow the momentum of the ceremony.

THE SEVEN BLESSINGS

Legally, only two witnesses must be present to make a valid marriage, but you need ten Jews—a *minyan*—to recite the seven blessings.

The *sheva b'rachot* are usually chanted in Hebrew by the rabbi or cantor, who might also read them in English, but translations can be read by family members or close friends either standing at their seats or under the *huppah*. You can also ask everyone to read in English from a wedding booklet, which creates a chorus of blessing.

Sheva b'rachot comprise the entire liturgy of the second part of the ceremony, yet their order can be confusing and some of the meaning obscure. For example, only two blessings have anything to say about weddings, and they come at the very end. Taken as a whole, however, the *sheva b'rachot* place the couple under the *huppah* at the very center of Jewish history and belief.

The seven blessings invoke some of the great themes of Judaism, including creation, peoplehood, Jerusalem, and redemption. They make every wedding the fulcrum of time, the center point between creation and redemption, between the first days and the end of days. All three of these archetypal moments—the beginning, your wedding, and the end—share the qualities of wholeness, sweetness, and the presence of God.

Jewish mystics saw the wedding as a metaphor for redemption and wholeness. After Eden, when humanity was exiled from *shalom*—from peace and completion— God's feminine self, *Shechinah*, also went into exile, wandering the earth, cut off and bereaved, except on Shabbat, when God and *Shechinah* unite, like the couple under the *huppah*. Judaism has no concept of individual redemption—no one enters paradise until everyone is

able to; the vision of redemption in the *sheva b'rachot* is a
taste of the time when humanity will be at peace and the
planet again becomes Eden. Which may be one of the reasons why weddings make us cry.

Because the language of the seven blessings reflects
ancient views of gender and same-sex couples have no
standing at all, many alternatives are available. Several are
included at the end of this section, along with an entirely
reimagined ceremony, *Brit Ahuvim*, Lovers' Covenant.

FIRST BLESSING

בָּרוּךְ אַתָּה יְיָ, אֱלֹהֵינוּ מֶלֶךְ הָעוֹלָם, בּוֹרֵא פְּרִי הַגָּפֶן.

*Blessed are You, Adonai our God, Ruler of the
Universe, who created the fruit of the vine.*

The first blessing is the second wedding *kiddush* and
serves as the liturgical introduction to those that follow.
The Talmud mentions only six wedding blessings, but ever
since the sixth century, Jews have made a practice of adding it and rounding the number up to seven: the number
of completion. The wine is not drunk until all seven blessings have been chanted.

SECOND, THIRD, AND FOURTH BLESSINGS

בָּרוּךְ אַתָּה יְיָ, אֱלֹהֵינוּ מֶלֶךְ הָעוֹלָם, שֶׁהַכֹּל בָּרָא
לִכְבוֹדוֹ.

Blessed are You, Adonai our God, Ruler of the Universe,
who created everything for Your glory.

בָּרוּךְ אַתָּה יְיָ, אֱלֹהֵינוּ מֶלֶךְ הָעוֹלָם, יוֹצֵר הָאָדָם.

Blessed are You, Adonai our God, Ruler of the Universe,
shaper of humanity.

בָּרוּךְ אַתָּה יְיָ, אֱלֹהֵינוּ מֶלֶךְ הָעוֹלָם, אֲשֶׁר יָצַר אֶת
הָאָדָם בְּצַלְמוֹ, בְּצֶלֶם דְּמוּת תַּבְנִיתוֹ, וְהִתְקִין לוֹ
מִמֶּנּוּ בִּנְיַן עֲדֵי עַד. בָּרוּךְ אַתָּה יְיָ, יוֹצֵר הָאָדָם.

Blessed are You, Adonai our God, Ruler of the Universe, who
has shaped humanity in Your image, patterned after Your image
and likeness, and enabled us to perpetuate this image out of our
own being. Blessed are You, Adonai, shaper of humanity.

These three blessings celebrate the ongoing process of
creation. The first, which blesses God for creating *hakol*,
"all things," recalls the story in Genesis where God makes
the "heavens and the earth and everything in them." In
this way, the creation of the universe and the creation of
your marriage are linked.

The next two blessings move from the creation of the universe (*hakol*) to the creation of humanity, and our unique place in that universe. The second blessing praises God for creating human beings, which takes place on the sixth day of creation, a day referred to in Genesis as "exceedingly good."

The third blessing begins as a repetition of the second, but continues by praising God for giving humanity the ability to perpetuate God's image and likeness "out of our own being." At a wedding, this can be understood as a benediction of love, marriage, sexuality, and generativity.

FIFTH BLESSING

שׂוֹשׂ תָּשִׂישׂ וְתָגֵל הָעֲקָרָה, בְּקִבּוּץ בָּנֶיהָ לְתוֹכָהּ
בְּשִׂמְחָה. בָּרוּךְ אַתָּה יְיָ, מְשַׂמֵּחַ צִיּוֹן בְּבָנֶיהָ.

*May the barren one exult and be glad as her
children are joyfully gathered to her. Blessed are You,
Adonai, who gladdens Zion with her children.*

This blessing extends the images of creation in terms of a mother surrounded by children. It promises that God will repeat the miracles given to Sarah and Rachel—barren women who were finally able to have children—and fulfill the biblical promise for the continuation of Zion, which is another name for the Jewish people.

Zion is also a synonym for Jerusalem, the holiest place on earth, where Adam was created and where the Temple stood. According to Midrash, when the Messiah arrives—in other words, when time comes to an end—the souls of all the Jews who ever lived will find their way to Zion. The fifth marriage blessing is a prayer for the redemptive unity of the end of days.

Alternatives to the fifth blessing retain the vision of redemption but avoid references to children and barrenness, which are not relevant and even painful to people who do not want or are unable to be (birth) parents.

FIFTH BLESSING ALTERNATIVES

Praised are you, Lord our God, who has given us a vision of the paradise we dream of creating with our lives and called it redemption. We praise you, O Lord, who created the commitment of marriage as a foretaste of redemption.

—RABBI RAMIE ARIAN

or

Blessed are You, Eternal our God, and Ruler of the World, who has set us apart through sacred obligations, and commanded us about the responsibilities of all humans for each other. You have forbidden exploitation and abuse, and permitted covenants of love. Blessed are You, Eternal One,

who makes your people Israel (all those who struggle with God)
holy with a huppah (a canopy of love and protection.)

—BY RABBI ELIOT ROSE KUKLA
AND RABBI JUSTIN LEWIS [14]

SIXTH AND SEVENTH BLESSINGS

שַׂמֵּחַ תְּשַׂמַּח רֵעִים הָאֲהוּבִים, כְּשַׂמֵּחֲךָ יְצִירְךָ בְּגַן עֵדֶן
מִקֶּדֶם. בָּרוּךְ אַתָּה יְיָ, מְשַׂמֵּחַ חָתָן וְכַלָּה.

Grant great joy to these loving companions
as You once gladdened your creations in the
Garden of Eden. Blessed are You, Adonai,
who gladden the bridegroom and the bride.

בָּרוּךְ אַתָּה יְיָ, אֱלֹהֵינוּ מֶלֶךְ הָעוֹלָם, אֲשֶׁר בָּרָא שָׂשׂוֹן
וְשִׂמְחָה, חָתָן וְכַלָּה, גִּילָה רִנָּה, דִּיצָה וְחֶדְוָה, אַהֲבָה
וְאַחֲוָה, וְשָׁלוֹם וְרֵעוּת, מְהֵרָה יְיָ אֱלֹהֵינוּ יִשָּׁמַע בְּעָרֵי
יְהוּדָה וּבְחוּצוֹת יְרוּשָׁלָיִם, קוֹל שָׂשׂוֹן, וְקוֹל שִׂמְחָה,
קוֹל חָתָן וְקוֹל כַּלָּה, קוֹל מִצְהֲלוֹת חֲתָנִים מֵחֻפָּתָם,
וּנְעָרִים מִמִּשְׁתֵּה נְגִינָתָם. בָּרוּךְ אַתָּה יְיָ, מְשַׂמֵּחַ חָתָן
עִם הַכַּלָּה.

Blessed are You, Adonai our God, Ruler of the universe,
who created joy and gladness, groom and bride, merriment,

song, dance and delight, love and harmony, peace and
companionship. Adonai our God, may there soon be
heard in the cities of Judah and the streets of Jerusalem
the voice of joy and the voice of gladness, the voice of the
bridegroom and the voice of the bride, the rapturous voices
of the wedded from their bridal chambers, and of young
people feasting and singing. Blessed are You, Adonai,
who gladden the bridegroom together with the bride.

In the last two blessings, the wedding couple finally make an appearance with the wish that they will be as happy as Adam and Eve, perfect partners made of the same dust. The phrase "loving companions" suggests the importance of both passion and friendship in marriage.

The sixth and seventh blessings end with references to the couple under the *huppah*. In the sixth *b'racha* they are referred to individually, in the seventh they are blessed together, suggesting the importance of individuality as well as union in marriage.

The seventh *b'racha* surrounds the couple with a chorus of rapturous voices, and Jerusalem, the center of the world, echoes with their joy. Given the economy of most rabbinic language, these ten synonyms for happiness are a remarkable testament to the moment. This catalog of happiness is the liturgical climax of the wedding and sets the stage for the *simcha* to follow.

Alternatives to these blessings widen the circle of joy to include same-sex couples, and in the seventh to enlarge the chorus of joy and love to include humankind "in all its variety."

> *Blessed are you, Faithful One, our God, sovereign of all worlds, who has created gladness and joy, loving partners, glee, song, mirth and exultation, harmony and love, and peace and companionship. Soon, eternal One, our God, may there be heard in the cities of Judah and in the streets of Jerusalem the voice of joy, the voice of gladness, the voices of loving partners from the huppah, and from celebrations festive songs of young friends. Blessed are you, joyful One, who brings loving companions together to rejoice in each other.*
>
> —RABBI'S MANUAL OF THE RECONSTRUCTIONIST RABBINICAL ASSOCIATION

After the blessings are completed, the couple drinks from the second cup of wine.

This is the moment when some rabbis speak directly to the couple about their relationship and their future, and when couples speak to each other. Despite there being no vows or *I do*s in the Jewish liturgy, there is an irrepressible need to say yes. While rabbis avoid language associated with Christian weddings ("to have and to hold"), many encourage couples to make personal promises to each other. (This can also be part of the *ketubah* reading earlier in the service.)

Some rabbis pose questions to the beloveds about their commitment to each other, to creating a Jewish home, and the like. The more a rabbi knows the couple, the more personal the questions can be: "Do you, Len, promise to laugh at Jessie's jokes, to go bird-watching once in a while, and to live together as companions and lovers?"

Finally, the rabbi announces that the marriage is legal according to the secular authorities and Jewish tradition: "By the power vested in me by the state of . . . and according to the traditions of Moses and Israel . . ."

SHATTERING THE GLASS

The ceremony ends with a famous bang. Stomping on a glass is one of the best-known features of Jewish weddings. Traditionally, the groom did the deed; today the couple often share the honor/pleasure, smashing one or two napkin-wrapped glasses.

Few Jewish symbols have a single explanation, and this one is downright kaleidoscopic. The custom dates back to the writing of the Talmud: "Mar bar Rabina made a marriage feast for his son. He observed that the rabbis present were very gay. So he seized an expensive goblet worth four hundred zuzim and broke it before them. Thus he made them sober."[15] In other words, where there is rejoicing, there should be trembling.

By the Middle Ages, synagogue facades in Germany were inlaid with a special stone for the express purpose of smashing a glass at the end of weddings. However, its interpretation changed somewhat by the fourteenth century, when it was viewed as a reminder of the destruction of the Temple in Jerusalem.[16] Either way, the lesson is that even at the height of personal joy, we recall the pain and losses suffered by the Jewish people and remember a world in need of healing.

The fragility of glass suggests the frailty of human relationships. Since even the strongest love is subject to disintegration, the glass is broken as a kind of incantation: "As this glass shatters, so may our marriage never break."

Loud noises are a time-honored method for frightening and appeasing demons that are attracted to beautiful and fortunate people, such as the happy couple beneath the *huppah*.

Marriage is a covenant, which in Judaism is made by breaking or cutting something. At Sinai, tablets were broken; at a wedding, broken glass "cuts" the covenant.

Breaking the glass also has sexual connotations, as it prefigures the release of sexual union, which is not only permitted to married couples but also required of them. For centuries breaking the glass implicitly symbolized breaking the hymen, which is why it was so important that the groom succeed.

The crash of glass ends the hush of mythic time under the *huppah*, and the world rushes in. Everyone exhales, claps, and shouts, "Mazel tov!" The celebration begins.

You can break any kind of glass: old, new, borrowed, or blue. Whatever you choose, it should be well wrapped to prevent injury. A heavy cloth napkin is standard, but you can buy a satin pouch or a velvet bag. (Artisans fashion mementos out of the shards.) While a lightbulb wrapped in a linen napkin might make a louder pop, it seems like a poor stand-in for such a rich and ancient symbol.

BRIT AHUVIM, LOVERS' COVENANT:
A REFORMULATION OF THE JEWISH WEDDING

Professor Rachel Adler's *Brit Ahuvim,* first published in 1998, is more reinvention than "alternative."[17] Even the most egalitarian Jewish wedding is grounded in ancient property law, with a symbolic purchase of the bride by the groom through *kinyan,* the ring ceremony. While the exchange of rings in a liberal Jewish wedding, a double-ring ceremony, looks and feels reciprocal, *kinyan* is still the model in use. This legalism does not matter to Jews who interpret *kinyan* as mutually enacted, with both parties "acquiring" one another. Likewise, contemporary *ketubot* make no mention of *kinyan* or any terms that would contradict the idea of an equal covenant or partnership. With *Brit Ahuvim,* Professor Adler grounds a new ceremony in halachic partnership law—*shutafut*—where agreements are mutual and shared.

In *Brit Ahuvim,* there is no declaration "Behold you are sanctified to me with this ring according to the laws of Moses and Israel," nor is there a *ketubah.* Instead, the couple symbolically ratify their love with a custom the Talmud calls *l'hatil b'kis,* literally "to put into one pouch." Instead of putting rings on each other's fingers, each partner places something of value into a pouch, and together they lift it up in the air.

Brit Ahuvim blends familiar customs, language, and melodies with new ideas, satisfiying the need for a meaningful connection to the past while validating the sanctity of equality within marriage, and of marriage equality for all.

OUTLINE OF A *BRIT AHUVIM* CEREMONY

Invocation: *Mi Adir*

Officiant's welcome and address

Blessing over wine

Reading of the *Brit Ahuvim* document* in Hebrew and English

L'hatil b'kis: Establishment of the partnership by placing symbols of each person's resources into a bag and jointly lifting it

Exchange of rings with a reading or a blessing, for example: *Blessed are you, God, Source of Life, who remembers your covenant and is faithful to your covenant and keeps Your word.*

The Seven Blessings

Shattering of the glass

Yichud

---

*See page 56 for the *Brit Ahuvim* text.

SEVEN BLESSINGS: TRANSLATIONS, ALTERNATIVES, AND READINGS

All translation is interpretation. The best translations are an artful compromise that respects the meaning, rhythm, and style of the original while creating something beautiful in its own right.

Every translation is a series of decisions: How should *Adam* be translated? "Man" is a perfectly correct rendering of the Hebrew, but so is "humankind." Why translate *Adonai* at all?

A strictly literal translation from Hebrew to English is virtually impossible since Hebrew nouns have gender, which requires changes in verb forms. Hebrew and English also deal with tenses very differently.

The examples on the following pages take a variety of approaches to the seven blessings. Some of the translations are relatively faithful to the original; some are almost entirely interpretive. The readings on page 154 can be used instead of a translation. Joel Rosenberg's "The Seven Blessings" on page 156 is a poem based on the text.

*Blessed are You, the boundless One, our God, sovereign
of all worlds, who creates the fruit of the vine.*

*Blessed are You, source of life, our God,
sovereign of all worlds, whose whole creation
testifies to Your glorious presence.*

*Blessed are You, kind One, our God, sovereign
of all worlds, who fashions human beings.*

*Blessed are You, imageless One, our God, sovereign
of all worlds, who has fashioned human beings in
Your image, patterning them in Your likeness, and
preparing them to share in the chain of life. Blessed
are You, beloved One, who fashions human beings.*

*May Zion, the heart of our people, rejoice in the
ingathering of all her children and all who join together
in loving relationships. Blessed are You, welcoming
One, who makes Zion rejoice with her children.*

*Make joyful these loving companions, O God—
even as You once in the Garden of Eden made
joyful Your first couple. Blessed are you, Delight,
who makes joyful these loving companions.*

*Blessed are You, Faithful One, our God, sovereign of
all worlds, who has created gladness and joy, loving*

partners, glee, song, mirth and exultation, harmony
and love, and peace and companionship. Soon,
eternal One, our God, may there be heard in the cities
of Judah and in the streets of Jerusalem the voice of
joy, the voice of gladness, the voices of loving partners
from the huppah, and from celebrations festive songs of
young friends. Blessed are You, joyful One, who brings
loving companions together to rejoice in each other.

—*RABBI'S MANUAL* OF THE RECONSTRUCTIONIST
RABBINICAL ASSOCIATION. USED WITH PERMISSION.

Blessed are You, God, Source of the world,
who creates the fruit of the vine.

Blessed are You, God, Light of life, who
created everything for Your glory.

Blessed are You, God, Spirit of all things,
who has created the human being.

Blessed are You, God, Foundation of every life, who
fashioned humanity in Your likeness, and prepared
for us a shape and form in Your image, from one
generation to the next and for all eternity. Blessed
are You, God, who has created human beings.

Zion will surely celebrate and exult in the coming
together of her children. Blessed are You, God,
who brings joy to Zion through her children.

*Give pleasure to these beloved companions as You did to
Your creation in the Garden of Eden so long ago. Blessed
are You, God, who makes the hearts of this couple rejoice.*

*Blessed are You, God, Source of the universe, who
has created each of these two people, their delight
and their happiness, their rejoicing and singing,
dancing and festivity, love and friendship, peace
and pleasure. O God, may the voices of this
celebration be heard in the streets of our cities
and the hills of our countryside. May the words
of this couple go out with gladness from their
wedding huppah, and may the music of their friends
and guests surround them. Blessed are You, God,
who brings joy to the hearts of this couple.*

—JANET BERKENFIELD.
USED WITH PERMISSION.

*Holy One of Blessing, Your Presence fills creation,
forming the fruit of the vine.*

*Holy One of Blessing, Your Presence fills creation, as
all creation reflects your splendor.*

*Holy One of Blessing, Your Presence fills creation,
giving life to each human being.*

*Holy One of Blessing, Your Presence fills creation,
You created man and woman in Your image, each
reflecting the image of God for the other forever. Holy
One of Blessing, You give life to every being.*

*How happy is she who thought herself childless and
then finds that her children gather to rejoice within her.
Holy One of Blessing, You make Zion
happy with her children.*

*May these cherished friends rejoice in joy as You
once rejoiced in Your creation of the Garden
of Eden. Holy One of Blessing, Your presence
radiates joy for the bride and groom.*

*Holy One of Blessing, Your Presence fills creation,
You created joy and gladness, bridegroom and bride,
delight, song, laughter and gaiety, love and harmony,
peace and friendship. May all Israel soon ring with
voices of gladness and joy, voices of bridegrooms and
brides, voices raised in joyful wedding celebrations,
voices lifted in festive singing. Holy One of Blessing,
Your Presence radiates for the bride and groom.*

—JOAN KAYE.
USED WITH PERMISSION.

SHEVA

*Blessed are You, God, Source of Life,
who creates the fruit of the vine.*

*Blessed are You, God, Source of Life,
everything reveals Your glory.*

*Blessed are You, God, Source of Life,
Creator of humanity.*

Blessed are You, God, Source of Life, who has created
the variety of humanity in the Divine image, and
entrusted us with the responsibility of building the
future. Blessed are You, God, creator of humanity.

May Zion rejoice in the uprooting of senseless
hatred from its midst. Blessed are You, God, who
causes Zion to rejoice through love of peace.

Blessed are You, God, Source of Life, who creates
joy and happiness, loving companions, gladness,
singing, joy, and delight, love in all its variety, the
jubilant voices of lovers from within their chambers,
the sounds of loving partners feasting and singing.
Blessed are You, who rejoices with lovers.

—RABBI AYELET S. COHEN AND
RABBI MARC J. MARGOLIUS.
USED WITH PERMISSION.

SEVEN READINGS FOR THE SEVEN BLESSINGS*

—1—

Our goal should be to live life in radical amazement . . .
to get up in the morning and look at the world in a way
that takes nothing for granted. Everything is phenomenal;
everything is incredible; never treat life casually. To be spir-
itual is to be amazed.

—Rabbi Abraham Joshua Heschel

---

* From the wedding of Elizabeth Gazin Schwartz and Ari Lev Fertig

—2—

Love doesn't just sit there, like a stone, it has to be made,
like bread; remade all the time, made new.

—Ursula Le Guin

—3—

Listen. To live is to be marked. To live is to change, to
acquire the words of a story, and that is the only celebration
we mortals really know.

—Barbara Kingsolver

—4—

Love does not consist of gazing at each other but in looking
outward together in the same direction.

—Antoine de Saint-Exupéry

—5—

In the flush of love's light
we dare be brave
And suddenly we see
that love costs all we are
and will ever be.
Yet it is only love
which sets us free.

—Maya Angelou

—6—

Let the vow of this day keep itself wildly and wholly
Spoken and silent, surprise you inside your ears
Sleeping and waking, unfold itself inside your eyes
Let its fierceness and tenderness hold you
Let its vastness be undisguised in all your days

—© Jane Hirshfield[18]

—7—

Blessed be joy and gladness, lover and beloved, mirth, glad
song, pleasure, delight, love, celebration, friendship, peace
and companionship. Let us soon hear in the streets of the
cities and the paths of the fields the sound of joy and
the sound of gladness, the voice of the lover and the voice
of the beloved, the cheers of the couple from their canopy
and of the youths from their song-filled feasts. Blessed is the
gladness of the couple, rejoicing together.

—Free translation of the Hebrew blessing

THE SEVEN BLESSINGS

Blessed is the One who plumps the grape
    and makes the vine a sapphire necklace
    curling through the humus of the vineyards
    in the summer dew,

and blessed is the One whose world is weighty
    like the crown of branches on the Tree of Life,

and blessed is the One who made the human being,
*   fashioned in the hands from humus*
*   like a lump of clay,*

and blessed is the One who gave the human,
*   humus-born, the light of breath and speech,*
*   and made, from out of one, a two:*
*   a lasting structure, formed and shaped*
*   (who married all with joining words,*
*   enjoining all to know about the nakedness*
*   that may and may not be uncovered,*
*   and about the promised ones whose touch*
*   must be postponed, and gave forth unreservedly*
*   companionship beneath the canopy, with words*
*   across the cup of wine)!*

Rejoice, rejoice, O devastated Lady!
*   Let Jerusalem rejoice! and let her womb*
*   grow plump with children, gathered in*
*   from wandering in other worlds,*
*   like letters yearning to be speech,*
*   and blessed is the One*
*   who plants the fruit of joy*
*   inside the citadel*
*   atop her highest hill,*

and dance and shout and sing, beloved friends,
*   for in your laughter and your kisses*
*   is the blessed One, who gave us*
*   evanescent bliss in ancient days,*

inside the walled-in Garden
watered endlessly by springs and mists,
and blessed is that One who gives
a taste of Eden to the bridegroom and the bride,

and blessed is the One who fashioned songs
and ululations, dervish spinnings, ecstasies,
prophetic tongues, and jokes and puns,
and double meanings and new teachings,
and renewal of the Teaching,
and the passion between lovers,
and affection between friends and kin,
and blessed is the One who gave us strength
and peace!

O quickly, quickly,
Nameless One of ours, give Judah
and the outskirts of Jerusalem
the voice of weddings! Marry
its inhabitants, and make us one
with them, and make us One
with You, and give us speech
and poetry and pledges! Plump
the grape for us to bless,
and give us feasts and melodies,
and make us drunk with You,
O blessed One, who are
both Bridegroom and a Bride!

—© JOEL ROSENBERG.
USED WITH PERMISSION.

After the *Huppah*

After the glass is broken, guests usually shout, "Mazel tov," and start singing "Siman Tov" ("A Good Sign") and "Od Yishama" ("It Will Be Heard"). The couple walks out of the *huppah*, to a quiet room that has been set aside for *yichud*.

YICHUD

Yichud (seclusion) is a ten-minute island of privacy and peace, time to exhale and embrace, time to prepare for the celebration ahead.

Yichud originated in ancient times, when marriages were consummated immediately after the wedding ceremony. That practice ended long ago, but the custom of seclusion continued as a signal that the couple had public sanction to spend time alone—something forbidden to unmarried couples in some traditional communities.

Yichud is still a kind of consummation. The word means "bringing to completion," and that's what happens during this short break from being the very public center of attention. During *yichud*, you can absorb and acknowledge everything that just happened—that you are, in fact and finally, married.

Yichud is also time to eat your first meal as a married couple, which is not only romantic but also practical. Because once you return to your family and friends, the greeting, hugging, laughing, and picture taking make it hard to get much more than a taste of the food you so carefully selected.

Some traditional foods are associated with *yichud*. Ashkenazi Jews served "golden soup"—chicken soup—an omen of prosperity. In some Sephardic communities, the custom was a meal of doves, symbolic of marital peace. But you should eat whatever you want. Ask the caterer to prepare a tasting tray, or ask your friends to provide a selection of your favorites, whatever they might be: chocolate pudding, taco chips, strawberries and cream . . .

Yichud makes it almost impossible to organize a traditional receiving line, which is a mixed blessing. Receiving lines allow families to greet the guests, parents get to bask in their children's happiness (*kvell*), and everyone has a chance to meet all the principals and match names and faces. "So *you're* Cousin Susan!" "This is the friend who flew in from Thailand!"

On the other hand, receiving lines can be an ordeal, especially at big weddings. For the guests the wait can be long, and there's only time to say a quick "Mazel tov"; the families get tired and hungry; and worst of all, it keeps the couple from the *simcha*. In a way, forgoing a receiving line keeps the emphasis where it belongs: on the joy and gladness of brides and grooms.

BLESSINGS FOR THE MEAL

A wedding meal is a *se'udat mitzvah*—a commanded celebration—which begins with *kiddush*, the blessing for wine, and the *motzi*, the blessing for bread—usually a large, elaborately braided loaf of challah, the egg-rich bread served on Shabbat and festivals.

To give these blessings is an honor, typically bestowed on parents, grandparents, siblings, children, or friends. They can also be shared, one saying the blessing in Hebrew, the other in English.

The blessing for wine,* which is part of virtually all Jewish celebrations:

בָּרוּךְ אַתָּה יְיָ, אֱלֹהֵינוּ מֶלֶךְ הָעוֹלָם, בּוֹרֵא פְּרִי הַגָּפֶן.

Baruch atah Adonai, Eloheinu Melech Ha-olam,
borei p'ree ha'gafen.
Holy One of Blessing, Source of the universe,
You form the fruit of the vine.

The all-purpose toast that follows is *L'chaim,* "To life."

The blessing for bread:

בָּרוּךְ אַתָּה יְיָ, אֱלֹהֵינוּ מֶלֶךְ הָעוֹלָם, הַמּוֹצִיא לֶחֶם מִן הָאָרֶץ.

---

* Or grape juice.

Baruch atah Adonai, Eloheinu Melech Ha-olam,
hamotzi lechem min ha'aretz.
Holy One of Blessing, Source of the universe,
who creates bread from the earth.

After the *motzi*, someone may say, *"b'teayavon,"* Hebrew
for "bon appétit."

Festive meals conclude with *birkat hamazon*, a series of
blessings, much of it sung or chanted. Praying the *birkat* is
called *benching* (from the Yiddish *benchen*, "to bless"), and
the blessings are usually printed in small booklets called
benchers. Wedding *benchers* also include the seven wedding
blessings, which are repeated at the end of the *birkat*.
The *birkat* and seven blessings can be included in your own
wedding booklet.

The *birkat* is full of praises and thanks to God for
sustaining life, for compassion, for nourishing the Jewish
people with food and Torah, and for many other blessings.
These are followed by petitions that begin with the word
Harachaman, "May the compassionate One," and ask for the
blessings of peace and prosperity and the well-being of one's
hosts; at a wedding, blessings for the couple may be added.

The seven blessings from the wedding liturgy are
repeated next, but this time, the blessing over wine is
read last.[19] The blessings can be read in English only, or
each *b'racha* can be shared between two people, reading
in Hebrew and in English. Alternately, you can invite six
guests to offer personal blessing or short readings. (For
some examples, see page 154.)

The final blessing over wine can be made using the cup or cups raised under the *huppah*. If you used two *kiddush* cups, wine from each can be poured into a third larger goblet. This "cup of blessing" can become part of your Passover seders in years to come, serving as Elijah's and/ or Miriam's cup, symbols of hope and redemption.

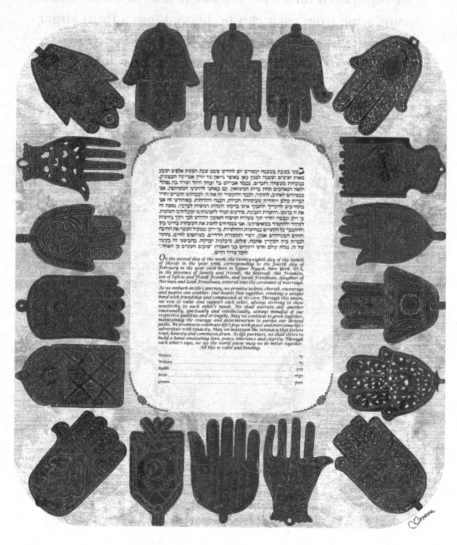

Hamsa Ketubah
© Temma Gentles
Image courtesy of www.ketubah.com

AFTERWARD

Newlyweds

Since biblical times, newly married couples had a special status in the community. Newly married men were exempt from military service, and Genesis makes reference to "the seven days of wedding celebration."[1]

That mention of seven days led to the custom of celebrating with newlyweds for a full week. Family and friends would bring food and end meals with *birkat hamazon* and, if one new person was present, repeat the seven wedding blessings.

Although the comparison may seem odd, these seven days mirror the seven (*shiva*) days of mourning after a death. According to folklore, both periods made people vulnerable to evil spirits; in the case of a death, the evil spirit might be called despair. When brides and grooms were barely acquainted before they married, they might have appreciated company during that first week. Although this custom continues in some communities, it has largely fallen out of use in favor of the honeymoon—which is in its own way acknowledgment and celebration of your new status as a married couple.

The whole first year of a marriage *is* different—even for couples that have lived together for years. When friends, acquaintances, and even complete strangers learn you are newlyweds, they smile and offer congratulations, and your happiness continues to brighten the world.

The special status of "bride" and "groom" lasts for a full year, a year of firsts: a first springtime and Passover seder, a first autumn and Rosh Hashanah. In other words, a year of creating—or perhaps redefining—your Jewish home together.

According to the Zohar, the central book of Jewish mysticism, God creates new worlds constantly by causing marriages to take place. These new worlds begin under the *huppah*, which is an outline, "its few lines a sketch for what might be." How you make that home, that new world, is your story to tell.

A Jewish Home

For generations, the definition of a Jewish home was straightforward: a place where two heterosexual Jews, a man and a woman, observed the laws of *niddah*, kept a kosher kitchen, posted *mezuzot* on the doorposts, observed Shabbat and the holidays, and belonged to a synagogue.

Today, there is no single definition. Instead of a list of requirements, there are questions. Is it a Jewish home if one of you is technically not Jewish? Is it a Jewish home if Shabbat candles are never lit, but those who live there volunteer unselfishly for social justice and Jewish causes? Is it a Jewish home if bacon is a Sunday-morning tradition? Is it a Jewish home if both are born Jews but neither ever gives the question a thought?

One *ketubah* describes the commitment to establishing a Jewish home as a pledge to be "open to the spiritual potential in all life wherein the flow of the seasons and the passages of life are celebrated through the symbols of our Jewish heritage. A home filled with reverence for learning, loving, and generosity. A home wherein ancient melody, candles and wine sanctify the table. A home joined ever more closely to the community of Israel."[2]

A Jewish wedding is an invitation to explore Judaism's wisdom as well as customs and laws, an exploration that begins or deepens during premarital meetings with your rabbi.

The Jewish home is sometimes called a *mikdash ma'at*— "a little sanctuary."

Sanctuaries feel different from places of business. Sanctuaries are suffused with peace and encourage a self-consciousness absent in most public spaces. The threshold of a *mikdash* creates a separation that defies the idea that all places are essentially the same, that space is empty of meaning.

Sanctuaries are visibly different from other places. They are filled with voices, sometimes reading in unison and sometimes raised in passionate debate. There is music in the sanctuary and occasionally the deep, living silence of a garden.

A sanctuary is a place of rest, safety, and asylum. Its doors are open.

No home is ever fully or finally a sanctuary. A *mikdash ma'at* is always a work in progress.

The keystone of a *mikdash ma'at* is Shabbat, the weekly island of peace and quiet created when we can step away from the demands and noise of the world and count our blessings. On Friday nights, the table ritual of candles, wine, and bread is a reminder of everything the world gives us while celebrating our ability to let go of it all.

In many households, Friday night Sabbath rituals include giving thanks directly to those we love, with prayers for children and praise for spouses. For centuries, husbands have recited or sung a poem to wives based on verses from Proverbs called *Eshet Chayil*—A Woman of Valor.

The language and assumptions of the traditional poem (see page 187) don't work for most couples today and alternative versions abound. Some couples simply take a moment to kiss and whisper a private endearment.

A SHABBAT BLESSING FOR BELOVEDS

The light in your eyes is more precious than rubies.
My heart is yours.
Your gifts to me are numberless.
The work of your hand enriches my life and the lives of
　　others.
You are like a burning candle, lighting our home with
　　vision and confidence, comfort and warmth.
I learn the Torah of love from your lips.
Our family and friends join me in saying,
"There are many fine people in the world; you are
　　extraordinary."
May all of your works bring you pleasure and fame, joy
　　and satisfaction, delight and happiness.
And may I be blessed to remain your partner in it all.[3]

Divorce

According to the Talmud, when a marriage is dissolved, "even the altar sheds tears." However, divorce has always been a fact of Jewish life and Jewish law.

A traditional Jewish divorce requires a formal document called a *get*, which is commissioned by the husband, delivered to the wife, and acknowledged by a *bet din*, a rabbinical court. While there are a few cases where a wife can obtain a *get* or compel her husband to give her one, divorce, like marriage, is essentially a male prerogative.

Jewish law holds that a woman who has not obtained a *get*—even if she has been granted a civil divorce—may not remarry as a Jew. She is called *agunah*—literally, "one who is chained"—and if she remarries, her children will be illegitimate (*mamzerim*) and may not marry Jews. These rules do not apply to men, who may refuse to grant a *get* and still remarry.

In the nineteenth century, the Reform movement responded to the inequity in these laws by discarding the *get* altogether and recognized civil divorce as a valid way to formally end Jewish marriages. This became the standard practice for the vast majority of Jews in North America. The Conservative movement, which considers itself bound by *halachah* (Jewish law), adopted a codicil to the *ketubah* called the Lieberman clause, which obliges couples that divorce to appear before a *bet din* to end their union according to Jewish law. (See page 60.) Similar language is sometimes included in *tenaim* documents.

Today, Jews of all denominations and descriptions have reclaimed and re-created Jewish ritual to end relationships that began under a *huppah*. Contemporary Jewish divorce practices and documents are reciprocal, with both partners granting each other permission to remarry and affirming a new start for themselves.

These kinds of divorce proceedings are often executed without a face-to-face meeting between the parties. When ceremonies are requested or required by a rabbi, they are private and brief: A rabbi might meet with the couple, each of whom brings a witness. The *get* is read aloud and signed, and following ancient tradition, the document is cut or torn to enact the dissolution of the marriage. If only one spouse is present, the *get* can be executed and delivered to the other for signing.*

---

* See www.ritualwell.org for ceremonies and documents.

LIBERAL *GET*

On the ___ day of the week, the ___ day of the month of
_____ five thousand seven hundred ___ years since
the creation of the world as we reckon here in _____
located near _____ daughter/son of _____ who
resides in _____ said to _____ son/daughter of
_____ I, of my own free will, grant you this bill of
divorce. I hereby release you from the contract, which
established our marriage. From today onward, you are
not my spouse and I am not your spouse. You belong to
yourself and are free to marry again.

  With this *Get*, I _____, free you, _____, from
all vows and commitments of marriage made under Jewish tradition.

  I turn to the source of life and love:

  Let me not pray to be sheltered from dangers, but to
be fearless in facing them.

  Let me not beg for the stifling of my pain, but for the
heart to conquer it.

  Let me not crave in anxious fear to be saved, but hope
for the patience to win my freedom.

  Give me the strength to make my love fruitful in service.

  Let hurt disappear and anger dissipate, and may I find
in my freedom the power to face all my tomorrows.[4]

MIKVEH

Immersion in a *mikveh* is another way to create closure. Whether or not you immersed at the beginning of your marriage, this ritual can embody the profound change as one chapter of your life ends and another begins.

MIKVEH CEREMONY FOLLOWING THE END OF A RELATIONSHIP*

Kavanah for preparation:

> *I stand here, having completed the unbinding of a*
> *   relationship.*
> *I stand here with dignity and with strength.*
> *I stand alone, a whole and complete person,*
> *   no longer bound as a companion and partner.*

or

> *For everything there is a season*
> *and a time for every purpose under heaven:*
> *A time to be born and a time to die,*
> *a time to plant and a time to uproot . . .*
> *a time for tearing down and a time for building up . . .*
> *a time for weeping and a time for laughing . . .*
> *a time for embracing and a time to refrain from*
> *   embracing.*

---

*Based on a ceremony created by the Mayyim Hayyim Ritual Team, 2004: Matia Rania Angelou, Deborah Issokson, and Judith D. Kummer. Used by permission. www.mayyimhayyim.org.

FIRST IMMERSION

Take a moment to reflect on what you have left behind. Immerse so that every part of your body is covered in the water. When you emerge, recite:

> Blessed are You, God, Majestic Spirit of the Universe,
> Who makes us holy by embracing us in living waters.

SECOND IMMERSION

Take a deep breath and exhale completely while gently and completely immersing for the second time. When you emerge, recite:

> May I turn toward the light.
> May I turn toward hope.
> May I turn toward new possibilities.

THIRD IMMERSION

Take a moment for personal reflection. When you emerge, recite:

> May I emerge from these living waters open and
>   refreshed,
> Strengthened to move forward.
> May I have the courage to accept what this journey will
>   bring.

Tay-Sachs and Allied Diseases

Tay-Sachs disease is one of several rare hereditary diseases that are far more common among Jews of Eastern European descent (Ashkenazi) than in the general population. The cause of Tay-Sachs is the absence of a vital enzyme called hexosaminidase A (Hex A), which the body uses to break down fatty substances (lipids) in the brain. Without the Hex A enzyme, lipids accumulate and eventually destroy brain function. By the age of about six months, a baby with Tay-Sachs disease loses physical skills, sight, and the ability to eat or smile. The disease has no known cure, and death usually occurs by the age of five.

Carriers of the Tay-Sachs gene do not have the disease themselves, but if two carriers conceive a child, chances are one in four that the baby will have it. A simple blood test can determine whether one is a carrier. Couples who find out both partners have the Tay-Sachs gene may choose to adopt rather than try to conceive, or to use egg donation or artificial insemination from noncarriers.

Amniocentesis, removal of a small quantity of fluid from the uterus early in the second trimester of pregnancy, can determine whether a fetus has Tay-Sachs, and if so, couples may choose to terminate the pregnancy.

Judaism takes a nuanced approach to abortion. Even

the narrowest interpretation of Jewish law allows abortion to save the life of the mother. If severe prenatal defects or genetic disease are evident in the fetus, Jewish law sanctions abortion not from the perspective of the child, but to spare the mother's pain over her child's suffering.

Genetic testing is strongly recommended for couples where both biological partners are of Ashkenazi descent. If both are carriers, rabbis can serve as a sounding board, a source of comfort, and provide referrals to thoughtful physicians, genetic counselors, and support groups.

For more information about Tay-Sachs and the other rare genetic diseases, contact:

The National Tay-Sachs and Allied Diseases Association, www.ntsad.org

The Center for Jewish Genetics, www.jewishgenetics.org

APPENDICES

BIRKAT HAMAZON, BLESSINGS AFTER THE MEAL (SHORT VERSION)

LEADER: Friends, let us praise God!

ALL: Praised be the name of God, now and forever.

LEADER: Praised be the name of God, now and forever.

Praised be our God, of whose abundance we have eaten.

ALL: Praised be our God, of whose abundance we have eaten, and by whose goodness we live.

LEADER: Praised be our God, of whose abundance we have eaten, and by whose goodness we live. Praised be the Eternal God.

ALL: Sovereign God of the universe, we praise You: Your goodness sustains the world. You are the God of grace, love, and compassion, the Source of bread for all who live, for Your love is everlasting. In Your great goodness we need never lack for food; You provide food enough for all.

We praise You, O God, Source of food for all who live.

As it is written: When you have eaten and are satisfied, give praise to your God who has given you this good earth. We praise You, O God, for the earth and for its sustenance.

Let Jerusalem, the holy city, be renewed in our time. We praise You, Adonai, in compassion You rebuild Jerusalem. Amen.

Harachaman, O Merciful One, be our God forever.

O Merciful One, heaven and earth alike are blessed by Your presence.

O Merciful One, bless this house, this table at which we have eaten.

O Merciful One, send us tidings of Elijah, glimpses of good to come, redemption and consolation.

O Merciful One, bless this company, and allow us all to gather soon and often for such joyous occasions.

May the Source of peace grant peace to us, to all Israel, and to all the world. Amen. May the Eternal grant strength to our people.

May the Eternal bless our people with peace.

ADDITIONAL *HARACHAMAN*
FOR A WEDDING

O Merciful One, bless Jessie and David with *shalom* in their hearts and under their roof.

O Merciful One, bless the parents of Jessie and the parents of David with many more years of joy and *naches* from their children.

O Merciful One, bless Jessie and David with a sense of humor in times of difficulty and with patience in times of distress.

TRADITIONAL/ORTHODOX DOCUMENTS

ORTHODOX *TENAIM*

TO A GOOD FORTUNE

May it come up and sprout forth like a green garden
whoso finds a wife finds a great good, and obtains favor
of the good Lord who ratifies this union.

May He who predestinates, bestow a good name and
future to the provisions embodied in this agreement,
which were agreed upon by the two parties hereto, that
is, as party of the first part, Mr. _____, who represents
the groom, Mr. _____, and as party of the second part,
Mr. _____, who represents the bride, Miss _____.

Firstly: That the above named groom agrees to take
himself as wife the above named bride, through huppah
and betrothal, in accordance with the Laws of Moses and
Israel; that they will neither abstract nor conceal from one
another any property whatsoever, but they shall equally
have power over their property, pursuant to the established custom.

The above named groom obligates himself to present
the bride with gifts according to custom.

The above named bride obligates herself to give as her
dowry the sum of _____ in cash, and clothes, pillows,
and linens, as is the custom.

The wedding will take place, if the Almighty so wills it, on the ___ day of _____ in the year _____ or sooner than such date if both parties agree thereto.

A fine is to be paid by the party breaking this agreement, to the other party, in the fixed sum of _____ and also in accordance with the laws of the land.

All of the foregoing was done with perfect understanding and due deliberation, and by means of the most effective method, in accordance with the ordinances of the sages, of blessed memory, and in accordance with the laws of the land; by means of striking hands, by solemn promises, by true affirmation, by handing over an object (from one contracting party to another), to take effect immediately; and this is not to be regarded as a mere forfeiture without consideration, or as a mere formula or document. We have followed the legal formality of a symbolic delivery (*kinyan*), by handing over an object, between the groom and the bride and their representatives, by using a garment legally fit for the purpose, to validate all that is stated above.

And Everything Is Valid and Confirmed.

ORTHODOX *KETUBAH*

On the ___ day of the week, the __ day of the month
_____ in the year five thousand seven hundred and
_____ since the creation of the world according to the
reckoning which we are accustomed to use here in the
city of _____ in _____. That _____,
son of _____ of the family _____, said to
this maiden _____, daughter of _____ of the
family _____, "Be my wife according to the law of
Moses and Israel, and I will cherish, honor, support, and
maintain you in accordance with the custom of Jewish husbands, who cherish, honor, support, and maintain their
wives faithfully. And I here present you with the marriage
gift of virgins, two hundred silver zuzim, which belongs
to you, according to the law of Moses and Israel; and I
will also give you your food, clothing, and necessities, and
live with you as husband and wife according to the universal custom." And _____ this maiden consented and
became his wife. The trousseau that she brought to him
from her father's house in silver, gold, valuables, clothing,
furniture, and bedclothes, all this _____ the bridegroom accepted in the sum of one hundred silver pieces,
and _____ the bridegroom consented to increase
this amount from his own property with the sum of one
hundred silver pieces, making in all two hundred silver
pieces. And thus said _____ the bridegroom, "The
responsibility of this marriage contract, of this trousseau,
and of this additional sum, I take upon myself and my

heirs after me, so that they shall be paid from the best part of my property and possessions that I have beneath the whole heaven, that which I now possess or may hereafter acquire. All my property, real and personal, even the shirt from my back, shall be mortgaged to secure the payment of this marriage contract, of the trousseau, and of the addition made to it, during my lifetime and after my death, from the present day and forever." _____ the bridegroom, has taken upon himself the responsibility of this marriage contract, of the trousseau and the addition made to it, according to the restrictive usages of all marriage contracts and the additions to them made for the daughters of Israel, according to the institutions of our sages of blessed memory. It is not to be regarded as an indecisive contractual obligation or as a mere formula of a document. We have followed the legal formality of symbolic delivery (*kinyan*) between _____ son of _____ and _____ daughter of _____ this maiden and we have used a garment legally fit for the purpose, to strengthen all that is stated above, and Everything Is Valid and Confirmed.

PRENUPTIAL AGREEMENT

In the event that the covenant of marriage entered into on the ___ day of _____, 20___, by _____ and _____, shall be terminated by the civil authorities, then _____ and _____ shall voluntarily and promptly upon demand by either of the parties present themselves at a mutually convenient time and place to terminate the marriage and release each other from the covenant of marriage in accordance with Jewish law and custom.

This agreement is recognized as a material inducement to the marriage by the parties hereto. Failure of either of the parties to perform the obligations hereunder if requested to do so by the other party shall render him or her libel for all costs, including attorneys' fees, reasonably incurred by the requesting party to secure his or her performance.

ORTHODOX *GET*

On the ___ day of the week, the ___ day of the month of
_____ in the year ___ from the creation of the world
according to the calendar reckoning we are accustomed
to count here, in the city _____, which is located on
the river _____ and _____, I do willingly con-
sent, being under no restraint, to release, to set free, and
put you aside, my wife _____ daughter of _____
who are today in the city of _____, which is located
on the river _____ and _____, who has been my
wife. Thus do I set free, release you and put you aside,
in order that you may have permission and the authority over yourself to go and marry any man you may desire.
No person may hinder you from this day onward, and you
are permitted to every man. This shall be for you a bill
of dismissal from me, a letter of release, and a document
of freedom, in accordance with the laws of Moses and
Israel.

ESHET CHAYIL—A WOMAN OF VALOR

*A woman of valor, who can find? Her value is far
beyond pearls. Her husband trusts in her and lacks
no fortune.*

*She repays his good, but not his harm, all the days of
her life.*

*She seeks out wool and linen, and her hands work
willingly.*

*She is like a merchant's ships; from afar she brings
sustenance.*

*She rises while it is still nighttime, and gives food to her
household and a ration to her maids.*

*She considers a field and buys it; she plants a vineyard
from the fruit of her handiwork.*

*She girds her loins with might and strengthens
her arms.*

*She knows her enterprise is good, her lamp is not
extinguished at night.*

*She puts her hands to the distaff, and her palms to the
spindle.*

*She spreads out her hands to the poor and extends them
to the destitute.*

*She does not fear the winter snow; her household is
clothed with scarlet wool.*

*She makes her family's bedcoverings; linen and purple
wool are her clothing.*

*Her husband is well known at the gates where he sits
with the elders of the land.*

She makes and sells garments and delivers a belt to the peddler.

Strength and splendor are her clothing, and she awaits her own end cheerfully.

She opens her mouth with wisdom, and the teaching of kindness is on her tongue.

She anticipates the needs of her household and has nothing to do with the bread of idleness.

Her children rise and celebrate her; her husband praises her.

"Many daughters have attained valor, but you have surpassed them all."

Grace is false and beauty is vain, but a God-fearing woman should be praised.

Give her the fruit of her hands, and she will be praised at the gates by her own deeds.

RESOURCES

Denominations Websites include information about marriage and weddings from their movement's point of view; some include links to local resources.

    Conservative: www.uscj.org

    Reconstructionist: www.Jewishrecon.org

    Reform: www.reformjudaism.org

    Renewal: www.alef.org

    Orthodox: www.chabad.com

Be'chol Lashon (In Every Tongue) An international advocate for Jewish diversity with educational materials and links to organizational partners, research, blogs, videos, programs, and some articles. www.bechollashon.org

Interfaith Family A website for intermarried families that includes information about weddings and Jewish life with links to articles, resources, blogs, discussion boards, organizations, and events in communities around the United States. www.interfaithfamily.org

Keshet A national organization that works for full LGBTQ equality and inclusion in Jewish life. The website includes articles about and rituals to help create inclusive weddings for LGBTQ couples and their allies. www.keshetonline.org

Mayyim Hayyim Living Waters Community Mikveh   Information about all things *mikveh* with resources for marrying couples and more. www.mayyimhayyim.org

Ritual Well   An online library of Jewish rituals, articles, documents, and prayers. www.ritualwell.org

THE JEWISH WEDDING NOW
KETUBAH ARTISTS

Mickie Caspi   www.caspicards.com

Rachel Deitsch   www.newworldketubah.com

Temma Gentles   www.temmagentles.com

Celia Lemonik   www.ketubah.com

Jennifer Raichman   www.jenniferraichman.com

Ginny Reel   www.ketubah-arts.com

Michelle (Shell) Rummel   www.ketubahtree.com

Robert Saslow   www.robertsaslowdesign.com

Diane Sidenberg   www.ketubbahart.com

NOTES

PART ONE: MARRIAGE IN JEWISH TRADITION

1. Philip Goodman and Hanna Goodman, *The Jewish Marriage Anthology* (Philadelphia: Jewish Publication Society of America, 1965), 44 (Zohar 1:89a).

2. Rabbi Maurice Lamm, *The Jewish Way in Love and Marriage* (San Francisco: Harper & Row, 1980), 128–29 (Yevamot 63b).

3. Goodman and Goodman, *Jewish Marriage Anthology*, 24 (Babylonian Talmud, Sotah 2a).

4. From *Pirke de Rabbi Eliezer,* trans. Gerald Friedlander (New York: Sepher-Hermon Press), 88; and Goodman and Goodman, *Jewish Marriage Anthology*, 34.

5. Goodman and Goodman, *Jewish Marriage Anthology*, 37 (Genesis Rabba 68:4).

6. Lamm, *Jewish Way*, 119.

7. Goodman and Goodman, *Jewish Marriage Anthology*, 30 (Bava Metzia 59a).

8. Ibid., 27 (Kiddushin 29b–30a).

9. 1 Samuel 1:8.

10. Isaiah 54:2.

11. Not all rabbis require *mikveh, milah,* and *bet din.*

12. Brenda Forster and Rabbi Joseph Tabachnik, *Jews by*

193

Choice: A Study of Converts to Reform and Conservative Judaism (Hoboken, NJ: Ktav Publishing House, 1991), 49.

PART TWO: CREATING YOUR JEWISH WEDDING

1. Lamm, *Jewish Way*, 179.
2. Abraham Joshua Heschel, *The Sabbath: Its Meaning for Modern Man* (New York: Farrar, Straus & Giroux, 1981), 8.
3. Ibid.
4. Goodman and Goodman, *Jewish Marriage Anthology*, 172.
5. Because the *huppah* symbolizes the marital bedroom, some Sephardic Jews do not do weddings in the sanctuary, near the Torah.
6. Rabbi Ayelet S. Cohen and Rabbi Marc J. Margolius.
7. Lamm, *Jewish Way*, 272.
8. Goodman and Goodman, *Jewish Marriage Anthology*, 90.
9. Moses Gaster, *The Ketubah* (New York: Sepher-Hermon Press, 1974), 20.
10. Ibid., 48.
11. Zalman Schachter-Shalomi with Donald Gropman, *The First Step* (New York: Bantam Books, 1983), 40.
12. Rachel Adler, *Engendering Judaism: An Inclusive Theology and Ethics* (Boston: Beacon Press, 1998), 169–209.
13. Sampson Raphael Hirsch, *Horeb* (London: Soncino Press, 1973), 533.

PART THREE: JOY AND GLADNESS

1. In addition to weddings, *se'udat mitzvah* follow celebrations for birth, adoption, bar and bat mitzvah, the completion of a course of Jewish study, and conversion to

Judaism. After a funeral, there is a meal of consolation
called a *se'udat havra'ah*.
2. From the *tenaim* ceremony by and for Rabbi Barbara
Rosman Penzner and Brian Penzner Rosman.
3. *Chaveirim Kol Yisraeil: In the Fellowship of All Israel; a Project
of the Progressive Chavurah Siddur Committee of Boston* (Ktav
Publishing House, 2000).
4. Samuel H. Dresner, *The Jewish Dietary Laws* (New York:
Burning Book Press, 1955), 19.
5. Hayyim Schneid, *Marriage* (Jerusalem: Keter Books,
1973), 42–43.
6. Ibid.
7. Ibid., 186.

PART FOUR: GETTING READY, HEART AND SOUL

1. Gerald Dicker, *Vehater Libeynu* (Purify Our Hearts),
prayer book of Congregation Beth El of the Sudbury
River Valley, Sudbury, MA (1980), 114.
2. Rabbi Burt Jacobson, "A Jewish Wedding Workbook."
3. Translation by Mark Frydenberg from *Chaveirim Kol
Yisraeil*.

PART FIVE: THE WEDDING DAY

1. Genesis 29:23–25.
2. Genesis 24:60.
3. Goodman and Goodman, *Jewish Marriage Anthology*, 28.
4. Jacobson, "Jewish Wedding Workbook," 60.
5. Jeremiah 31:22.
6. Lamm, *Jewish Way*, 214.
7. Hosea 2:19–20.
8. Author unknown. The seven circles represent seven *sefirot*

or sacred attributes: *chesed, gevurah, tiferet, netzach, hod, yesod, malchut.*

9. Translation by Debra Cash. In Hebrew, "bride and groom."

10. This is a more literal translation of the *erusin* blessing: "Blessed are You, Lord our God, Master of the Universe, Who has sanctified us with His commandments and commanded us regarding forbidden unions, and Who forbade to us betrothed women and permitted to us those we have married through *huppah* and *kiddushin.* Praised are You, Lord, Who sanctifies His people Israel with *huppah* and *kiddushin.*"

11. *Rabbi's Manual of the Reconstructionist Rabbinical Assembly.*

12. Rabbi Elliot Kukla and Rabbi Justin Jarod Lewis.

13. Rabbi Wolli Kaelter of Long Beach, California.

14. Used by permission of the authors.

15. Goodman and Goodman, *Jewish Marriage Anthology,* 97.

16. Lamm, *Jewish Way,* 229.

17. Adler, *Engendering Judaism,* 169–208. Rabbi Ami Adler (son of Rachel Adler) and Rabbi Julie Pelk Adler created *Brit Ahuvim* 2.0, described in a blog post that presents a *halachic* update and argues for its widespread adoption. therabbisadler.blogspot.com, July 2012.

18. "A Blessing for a Wedding," in Jane Hirshfield, *Come, Thief* (New York: Knopf, 2011), Used by permission of the author, all rights reserved.

19. According to *halachah,* only men are permitted to chant the *sheva b'rachot* under the *huppah* and following the wedding feast. However, women in traditional communities sometimes add their voices by reciting *sheva shevahot*—seven praises—before the meal. The *shevahot* make reference to women in the Bible, including Miriam, who gathered the women of Israel to celebrate

the Exodus from Egypt, and Deborah, who judged and
claimed victories in poems and songs.

AFTERWARD

1. Deuteronomy 24:5 and Genesis 28:27.
2. From a *ketubah* created by Rabbi Gustav Buchdahl, Rabbi
   Lawrence Kushner, Rabbi Eugene R. Lipman, and Rabbi
   Bernard H. Melhman.
3. By Anita Diamant, based on a version by Rabbi David
   Kline.
4. Text by Rabbi Leigh Lerner.

GLOSSARY

AGUNAH   Literally, "a chained woman": one whose marriage has not been terminated according to Jewish law and who is thus prohibited from remarrying.

ALEPH-BET   Name of the Hebrew alphabet; also, its first two letters.

ALIYAH   Literally, "to go up": to be called to the Torah. Also, "making *aliyah*" refers to moving to the land of Israel.

ARAMAIC   Semitic language closely related to Hebrew; the lingua franca of the Middle East. The Talmud was written in Aramaic, as are traditional legal documents, including *ketubah*, *tenaim*, and *get*.

ASHKENAZI   Jews and Jewish culture of Eastern and Central Europe.

AUFRUF   Recognition of a wedding couple at synagogue services.

BAAL SHEM TOV   Israel ben Eliezer, founder of Hasidism, eighteenth-century mystical revival movement.

BADCHAN   Master of ceremonies at a wedding celebration.

BARUCH ATA ADONAI ELOHEYNU MELECH HA'OLAM   Words
that begin Hebrew blessings, commonly translated,
"Blessed art Thou, Lord our God, King of the
Universe."

BCE   Before the Common Era. Jews avoid using the Christian
designation BC, which means "before Christ."

BEDEKEN   Ritual ceremony of veiling the bride before the
wedding ceremony.

BET DIN   Rabbinical court of three rabbis.

BIMAH   Raised platform in the synagogue, dais.

BRIS/BRIT   Covenant. *Bris* and *brit milah* refer to the covenant
of circumcision.

CE COMMON ERA.   Jews avoid the designation AD, which
means "in the year of our Lord."

CHALLAH   Braided loaf of egg-rich bread, traditional for Shabbat, holidays, and festive occasions.

CHOSSEN   Yiddish for "groom"; in Hebrew, *hatan.*

CHOSSEN'S TISH   Literally, "groom's table": the name of the
celebration for the groom and his friends prior to
the wedding ceremony.

CONSERVATIVE   Religious movement, developed in the
United States during the twentieth century as a more
traditional response to modernity than that offered by
Reform.

DAVEN   Pray.

D'RASH   Religious insight, often on a text from the Torah.

D'VAR TORAH   Literally, "words of Torah": an explication about a portion of the Torah.

ERUSIN   Betrothal blessing and ceremony.

FLEISHIG   Meat food, which, according to *kashrut*, may not be mixed with dairy products.

FREILACH   Yiddish for "happy"; up-tempo songs.

GET   Formal document of Jewish divorce.

HALACHAH   Jewish law.

HASIDISM   Eighteenth-century mystical revival movement that stressed God's immanence in the world. The doctrine of *simcha*, "joy," was expounded as a way of communing with God.

HATAN   Hebrew for "groom"; in Yiddish, *chossen*.

HAVDALAH   Hebrew for "separation": the Saturday-evening ceremony that separates Shabbat from the rest of the week.

HAVURAH   Literally, "fellowship": small, intimate participatory groups of Jews who meet for prayer, study, and celebration.

HAZZAN   Cantor. *Hazzanit* is the female form.

HUPPAH   Wedding canopy.

KADDISH   Mourner's prayer.

KALLAH   Hebrew for "bride."

KASHRUT   System of laws that govern what and how Jews eat.

KETUBAH   Marriage contract.

KIDDUSHIN   Sanctification: a name for the betrothal and ring ceremony.

KITTEL   White robe worn under the canopy.

KLEZMER   A form of Jewish music.

KOSHER   Permissible to be eaten according to the laws of *kashrut*; also, proper, legitimate.

MACHETUNIM   The relationship between in-laws. "The parents of my son-in-law are my *machetunim*."

MAVEN   An expert.

MAZEL TOV   Literally, "Good luck"; more generally, "Congratulations."

MENSCH   Person; an honorable, decent person.

MESADER KIDDUSHIN   One who "orders" or leads the marriage ceremony.

MEZUZAH   First two paragraphs of the Shema written on a parchment scroll and encased in a small container, to be affixed to the doorposts of a home.

MIDRASH   Imaginative exposition of the Hebrew bible.

MIKVEH   Ritual bath.

MILCHIG   Dairy foods, which, according to *kashrut*, may not be mixed with meat products.

MINHAG   Custom.

MINYAN   Group of ten adult Jews, the minimum for community prayer.

MISHEGAS   Foolishness.

MITZVAH   Commandment; a good deed (pl., *mitzvot*).

MIZRACHI   Jews of the Middle East and North Africa.

MOTZI   Blessing over bread recited before meals.

NACHES   Special joy from the achievements of one's children.

NIDDAH   Rules regarding monthly *mikveh* practice, also ritually prepared.

NIGGUN   Wordless melody.

NISSUIN   Ceremony of the nuptials.

ONEG SHABBAT   Literally, "Sabbath delight." The informal meal or snack that follows Friday-night or festival services.

ORTHODOX   The Modern Orthodox movement developed in the nineteenth century in response to the Enlightenment and Reform Judaism. As with liberal Judaism, Orthodox is not monolithic.

PARASHA   Weekly Torah portion.

RABBI   Teacher. "The rabbis" refers to the men who codified the Talmud.

RECONSTRUCTIONIST   Religious movement, begun in the United States in the twentieth century by Mordecai Kaplan, that views Judaism as an evolving religious civilization.

REFORM   Movement, begun in nineteenth-century Germany, that sought to reconcile Jewish tradition and thought with modernity and the Enlightenment.

SCHMOOZE   Friendly chatter.

SEPHARDI   Jews from Spain, Portugal, and the Mediterranean.

SHABBAT   Sabbath.

SHADCHAN   Matchmaker.

SHECHINAH   God's feminine attributes.

SHEHECHEYANU   Prayer of thanksgiving for new blessings.

SHEVA B'RACHOT   Seven marriage blessings; first recited under the canopy, and following meals for seven days when a *minyan* is present.

SHIDDUCH   Marriage match.

SHOFAR   Ram's horn, blown during the High Holidays.

SHTETL   Small town, especially one inhabited by Ashkenazi Jews before the Holocaust.

SHUL   Synagogue.

SIDDUR   Daily and Shabbat prayer book.

SIMCHA   Joy and the celebration of joy.

SOFER   Ritual scribe.

TAHARAT HAMISHPACHAH   Laws of family purity prescribing women's sexual availability and the use of *mikveh*, also referred to as *niddah*.

TALLIS   Prayer shawl (pl., *tallisim*). Alternative spellings: tallit, tallitot.

TALMUD   Encyclopedic compilation of rabbinic thought, lore, and law consisting of the *Mishnah* and *Gemarah*, completed around the fifth century CE.

TENAIM   Literally, "conditions": formal engagement contracts; also, the name of the celebration that attends the signing of the document.

TORAH   First five books of the Hebrew Bible, portions of which are read every Shabbat.

TZEDAKAH   Charity; righteous action toward the poor and the repair of the world.

YICHUD   "Seclusion": brief period immediately following the marriage ceremony for the couple to be alone with each other.

YIDDISH   Language spoken by Ashkenazi Jews; combination of early German and Hebrew.

YIDDISHKEIT   Jewishness.

ZOHAR   Literally, "splendor": thirteenth-century text of Jewish mysticism.

ACKNOWLEDGMENTS

I have written acknowledgments for this book three times: for two editions of *The New Jewish Wedding* and here for *The Jewish Wedding Now*.

Reading acknowledgments from the past is a little like leafing through a photo album begun more than thirty years ago. New names appear in each edition, several were helpful in all three. Everyone was generous with time, insight, knowledge, and opinions, and I am grateful to all.

For *The Jewish Wedding Now*, I had conversations and correspondence with Rabbi Lev Baesh, Lisa Berman, and Carrie Bornstein of Mayyim Hayyim Living Waters Community Mikveh (www.mayyimhayyim.org); Janet Buchwald, Rabbi Ayelet S. Cohen; Daniel Bahner and Jordyn Rozensky of Keshet (www.keshet.org); Rabbi Roni Handler of Ritual Well (www.ritualwell.org); Rabbi Suzie Jacobson; Rabbi Elliot Kukla; Rabbi Justin Jaron Lewis; Rabbi Suzanne Offit; Elizabeth Schwartz and Lev Fertig; Rabbi Becky Silverstein; Cantor Rachel Stock Spilker; and Cantor Lorel Zar-Kessler. Thanks to all of the *ketubah* artists whose works beautify this book, especially Jennifer Raichman for the illustration details throughout. Kevin Lay at ketubah.com was a great help, as was Ineke Ceder for her careful eye. I am grateful to Debra Cash, Jane Hirshfield, and Joel Rosenberg for permission to reprint their works.

For *The Jewish Wedding Now*, I was especially fortunate in having Roz Lippel as my editor at Simon & Schuster; supportive and helpful, she is the reason this edition is so beautiful.

As in earlier editions, conversations with Rabbi Sharon Kleinbaum, Rabbi Noa Kushner, and Rabbi Michael Lezak provided new perspectives and insights. And once again, I relied on Rabbi Barbara Penzner, who was the very first person I interviewed for the first edition of *The New Jewish Wedding*. She became a primary resource, sounding board, reader, commentator, and informal editor for that book and my next five Jewish guidebooks and their subsequent revisions. She is a wise and wonderful rabbi friend. Credit is due to her succinct chapter on Jewish weddings in *A Guide to Jewish Practice, Volume 3—the Life Cycle*, published by the Reconstructionist Rabbinical College Press in 2014.

This book was, is, and always will be dedicated to Jim Ball, beloved, friend, and most patient of husbands.

I would never have thought to write it were it not for Rabbi Lawrence Kushner, who, when I asked him what I should read in preparation for our wedding, wheeled around from the bookshelf behind his desk, pointed a finger at me, and said, "You should write a book about Jewish weddings." From that point on, Larry acted as official godfather to this endeavor. He was (after Jim) the first reader of every chapter. His contributions were invaluable. His influence is pervasive. He has been and remains one of the great teachers of my life.

Arthur Samuelson was the first editor who understood the need for *The New Jewish Wedding* and helped refine its shape and voice. From that first edition, I remain indebted to Penina Adelman, Michele Alperin and Steven Sherriff, Rabbi Rebecca Trachtenberg Alpert, Rabbi Ramie Arian, Rabbi Al Axelrad, Rabbi Nina Beth Cardin (then at the Jewish Women's Resource Center, National Council of Jewish Women New York Section), Mickie Caspie, Debra Cash, Pattie Chase, Howard Cooper, Lev Friedman, Rabbi Everett Gendler, Rabbi Stuart Geller, Rabbi Susan Grossman, Rabbi Burt Jacobson, Joshua Jacobson, Rabbi Cherie Kohler-Fox, Jonathan Kremer, Cantor Riki Lippitz, Billy Mencow, Peggy McMahon, Larry Moulter, Rosie Rosenzwieg, Reb Zalman Schachter-Shalomi, Rabbi John Schechter, Rabbi Drorah Setel, Rabbi Daniel Shevitz, Rabbi Jeffrey Summit, Ella Taylor, Rabbi Max Ticktin, Rabbi Moshe Waldoks, and Rabbi Arthur Waskow.

For the 2001 update, I had help and support from Professor Rachel Adler, Ari Davidow, Rabbi Lisa Edwards, Rabbi Laura Geller, Rabbi Leigh Lerner, Rabbi Carl Perkins, Rabbi Joel Sisenwine, and Rabbi Liza Stern.

i carry it in my heart

i carry your heart

בשני בשבת בעשרים וכודרים יום לחודש שבט שנת חמשת אלפים ושבע מאות ושמנים לבריאת עולם למנין שאנו מנין כאן באפר נייאק ניו יורק אמריקה הצפונית, בטחות משפחה וחברים,
נכנסו אברהם בר יצחק ורחל שרדה בת נעמלי ולאה הנאהבים תחת בית הנישואין. עם צאתנו לדרכנו הנישואית, אנו פטוחים לאהוב, לחבק, לעודד ולהעניש זה את זה.
לבבותינו מאוחדים יחדיו לבריות עולם יחודית שבחסדרה חברות, הבנה יהודיות. באיחודנו זה אנו פטוחים להעריך ולתמוך זה את זה, ותמיד נשתדל ותקהות לזה.
לבצרכינו, נולדולגם זה את זה ברגש, יוחנית וחכמה, מורעים תמיד לתכונותינו ומעלותינו השונות, מי יותן ונצבתם יחיד מ שעותיה הארות של הצרות.
כאשפותינו, אנו מבשחיים לחגוג את השפחמות בחויד בכה להתות את החזקה והחמצה תעצומדרי אמון, וישר ותקושרה
תורים. בשותפים לחיים, נחתוד לבנות בית המקנהים אהבה, שלום, סובלנות וצדקה, בעיניהם של זה מדין, נגלה עולם חדש רותהים בנ האמר.
ויהי שריר וקיום.

On the second day of the week, the twenty-eighth day of the month of Shevat in the year 5768, corresponding to the fourth day of February in the year 2008 here in Upper Nyack, New York, U.S.A. in the presence of family and friends, the beloveds Abe Franklin, son of Sylvia and Frank Franklin, and Sarah Freedman, daughter of Norman and Leah Freedman, entered into the covenant of marriage

As we embark on life's journey, we promise to love, cherish, encourage and inspire one another. Our hearts fuse together, creating a unique bond with friendship and compassion at its core. Through this union, we vow to value and support each other, always striving to show sensitivity to each other's needs. We shall nurture one another emotionally, spiritually and intellectually, always mindful of our respective qualities and strengths. May we continue to grow together, maintaining the courage and determination to pursue our desired paths. We promise to celebrate life's joys with grace and overcome life's adversities with tenacity. May we maintain the intimacy that fosters trust, honesty and communication. As life partners, we shall strive to build a home emanating love, peace, tolerance and charity. Through each other's eyes, we see the world anew: may we be better together.
All this is valid and binding.

Witness _____ עד
Witness _____ עד
Rabbi _____ הרב
Bride _____ הכלה
Groom _____ החתן

I Carry Your Heart Ketubah
© Michelle "Shell" Rummel
Image courtesy of www.ketubah.com

PERMISSIONS

INDEX

213

ABOUT THE AUTHOR

Anita Diamant is the author of five novels and six guidebooks to contemporary Jewish life. Her bestselling fiction includes *The Boston Girl, The Red Tent, Day After Night, The Last Days of Dogtown,* and *Good Harbor. The Red Tent,* based on the biblical story of Dinah, has been published in more than twenty-five countries and was adapted for television by Lifetime TV.

Diamant's nonfiction guides include *The New Jewish Baby Book, Living a Jewish Life, Choosing a Jewish Life, How to Raise a Jewish Child,* and *Saying Kaddish.*

She has written for the *Boston Globe,* the *Wall Street Journal, Real Simple, Parenting, Hadassah Magazine, Reform Judaism,* and *Boston Magazine.* Personal essays from her newspaper and magazine columns are collected in *Pitching My Tent.*

Diamant grew up in Newark, New Jersey, and Denver, Colorado. She lives in the Boston area and is the founding president of Mayyim Hayyim Living Waters Community Mikveh, a twenty-first-century reinvention of the ritual bath as a place for exploring ancient traditions and enriching contemporary Jewish life.

For more information, visit www.anitadiamant.com.